To my family, fiancée, friends and colleagues who witnessed and nurtured my passionate political opinions from the tender age of 12! Thank you.

# THE MEANS TO
# A CHOSEN END

*Silvio Guadagnino*

*AuthorHouse™*
*1663 Liberty Drive, Suite 200*
*Bloomington, IN 47403*
*www.authorhouse.com*
*Phone: 1-800-839-8640*

*First published by AuthorHouse     6/10/2008*

*ISBN: 978-1-4343-8401-0 (e)*
*ISBN: 978-1-4343-8403-4 (sc)*

*Library of Congress Control Number: 2008903645*

*Printed in the United States of America*
*Bloomington, Indiana*

*This book is printed on acid-free paper.*

# Contents

# *This War and All Wars*

THE IRAQ WAR AND its repercussions can be felt throughout the world like a constant wave crashing the shore, slowly eroding its very existence at the disbelief of all those who watch its destruction right before their very eyes. So how do individuals get to the point where they feel and believe that they cannot stop the juggernaut that is ravaging the very soul of their people and all peoples, as its very nature consumes first the bodies, then the minds, and ultimately the souls of those who lie in the path of the crushing waves?

Perhaps the means to its ending comes from the understanding of the Iraq war's origins and undoubtedly its parallels to past conflicts. Regardless, what fueled this fire, what "oil" was added to cause the explosive effect it now has on society? Is it so simplistic to ascribe the turmoil, loss, and pain and suffering to a simple lack of understanding, or perhaps the lack of transparency, of the people by those in power? Would it not be so different from the past? Or would it?

I believe that in order to understand what actions must be taken, we must dissect and understand the scope and the landscape of the current political climate, and then and only then can we choose the right paths for our governments to follow in order to ensure the best interests of all people, as there is no defining line or border that cannot be penetrated on the road to victory. Otherwise we will all undoubtedly fall and feel the crushing blows of the ocean's fury.

This book will follow the path to better understand the factors involved, the many variables and their intensity on the final decision. By doing so, those variables, upon which the conflict is most dependent, can be massaged to produce the most desirable effect.

# CHAPTER 1

# *Win, Lose, or Draw*

BEFORE ANY PLANS ARE even laid out, a decision must be taken by the present and future US administrations as to whether the Iraq war is one that should end in victory or succumb to defeat. Basically, the White House and the government as a whole must choose whether the US is to win, lose, or draw in Iraq!

This essential factor will dictate the ferocity and intensity of the offensive America will have to wage and more importantly will influence the psychological warfare required to win the battles and attract allies to an otherwise defunct war.

Firstly, no government will openly admit to choosing defeat over victory or even mediocrity for that matter, but again actions speak louder than words. But what actions would echo the will and desire for victory? What actions could ignite the fire required to win the battles and ultimately the war?

Those actions can only come from the will of a united people represented by a united government. As the Republicans and Democrats will almost undoubtedly diverge in their approaches to the war, for or against, a common ground will have to be reached regarding other key issues that can be pursued in a bipartisan manner.

Firstly, a rough timeline must be laid out and accepted that extends beyond a few months. The rough timeline must be one measured in years such that the enemy will not be able to pool resources for the offensive that would be launched over the remaining months. Here is a case where one battles patience with patience, just as the Roman armies patiently waited for the enemy to crumble after cutting off all supply lines. There is simply no way around this fact, and if one were to admit the inevitable, 5 to 10 years would be required.

Within the first year, 2007–2008, every possible attempt must be made by the administration to persuade the UN and in particular the other nations to provide both the financial and military assistance required to lessen the burden currently carried by American forces stationed in the region. US government emissaries must explain the context of a postwar Iraq that could be the hub of terrorist activities and organizations around the world.

The only way to entice the allies around the world to assist in the exercise is to convey the possible scenarios that could result if such a situation were to materialize. Explain—better yet, implant—the seed of doubt regarding their proximity to the region that would make attacks on certain nations very probable and simpler should a plan be conceived.

Furthermore, one must not forget the underlying fact that the enemy will not disappear despite a US victory or defeat. The point of no return was passed the night that President Bush granted permission to drop the first bomb on Baghdad. The world cannot rescind that order, though it wishes it could.

So how does one choose an ending? Simple, one must believe in the outcome prior to its realization! At the very start of the war, back in 2003, victory was not only expected, it was as if history books were being written in advance of the outcome. Had that form of thought continued throughout the campaign to date, the current state of affairs would be drastically different.

Note that as America's armed forces were steaming ahead through Iraq back in 2003 on their way to Baghdad, the resolve was intense and the belief was undeniable regardless of the reasons for its inception. But then as the campaign wore on, the people began to second-guess the need for the war and its very reason, and doubt then crept into the equation. This dormant fact is what led to the perishing of America's best in distant desert settings. It was that very thinking that gave birth to the steady decline in America's influence and control and the current resurgence of terrorist forces over both the land and the people. This idea actually tipped the balance from belief to despair, draws its very energy from within, and is the weight now fully carried by the brave men and women of the armed forces.

Furthermore, this notion was further compacted into the minds of the masses as parallels to Vietnam began to appear, as though that war had been "reborn"—better yet, reincarnated and implanted within the bounds of a new and dangerous setting.

So how does one escape the traps of the human psyche? One cannot, unless one consciously and subconsciously decides to. Such actions were believed to have been taken by the government as it evaluated certain personnel as the root causes of the failing campaign. From then on, some of the major characters of this grand opera were replaced by their understudies, thereby changing the flavor of the presentation and the management of its operation. Those characters included everyone from Secretary Powell, who provided the desperately needed psychological/

political support for the campaign, to Secretary Rumsfeld, whose management style left a bitter taste on the palates of many on the hill, all the way to the soldiers minding the "Road of Death" leading to Baghdad airport.

The truth of it all is that the current situation can be compared to an eroding shoreline with a tide slowly growing in momentum and continuously extracting one layer at a time and in essence extracting its very soul! What once was will no longer be, all because of the mindset affected by the wave originating both from Iraq and unquestionably from Washington.

The next question one would and should ask would inevitably be posed by a child as an elder recites an explanation of the situation. That very action would give rise to a childlike yet highly intuitive question: "Why aren't we winning?" Such a simple question and yet so layered; so deceivingly simple and yet so complex!

To this question, one must stand back and search for the intuitive yet hidden answer. As Einstein says, "The simplest answer is the best, but don't oversimplify," leading to an incredible conclusion. America's ultimate decision is to either win, lose, or draw.

# CHAPTER 2

# *Who to Blame*

IN ORDER TO ARRIVE at an ending, whether chosen or forced upon, requires a succession of definite actions aligned with several spur-of-the-moment decision that resulted in the current situation, thereby dictating a future course of action. Despite this complicated web of decisions, with its numerous opaque layers lining the floor plans, one can still dissect the origins and the initial push of those who anticipated an outcome and aided in its initial acceptance, which transferred the idea from paper to reality. In all fairness, these same people unquestionably planned for the advancement of US policy, power, and hold over one of the most lucrative and crucial sections of the world. They by no means expected the outcome that is currently taking place within the region as described and seen in every major newspaper and newscast worldwide. These plans were in fact most probably part of an even grander agenda that would see the US controlling an ever-growing segment of the Middle East. Now, had the tides turned in the US's favor, despite the fierce opposition,

American power would have reached heights paralleled only during the Roman Empire, but as is all too obvious, the ocean's fury took hold and led the US on a completely different course. With this in mind, one has to analyze the situation in the context of the current setting and the actions to be taken in order to produce a chosen end. This task can be completed and accepted by all only after reviewing past actions and assigning blame to whomever created the turmoil and death that exists, such that the people can then decide who can properly manage the mounting heaps of problems resulting from the decision to wage war in Iraq.

This chapter's purpose is rather harsh, in that its raison d'etre is clearly aimed at the allocation of failure to all those who aided in producing the situation prevalent in Iraq. It will therefore serve as a spotlight upon the many characters involved but in turn will continually provide and make reference to these persons' ability to bring positive change and, more importantly, concrete actions, such that the final act is one that has been planned and will best suit American and allied interests.

When assigning blame, there is certainly no limit to the number of individuals that can and/or will be dragged down by the attention and limelight aimed in their direction. Regardless of the magnitude, one must focus the lens properly so that the key participants and decision makers involved are carefully and methodically scrutinized, as the majority of subordinates in the food chain are simply obeying orders. As the war was and is of the greatest importance, it thereby received the utmost attention by all; leading to the ultimate decision and final declaration for war, directly from the highest office in the land. This presidential order from the commander-in-chief is the launching pad from which everything has originated, and thus President Bush inherits all the failure associated with the current situation. Conversely, had the US been successful, he would have basked in the glory; but as time showed, it was not meant to be. If one goes through the actions undertaken by this president, all the while noting the other key players that agreed or disagreed with his position, it becomes obvious that proper action was not taken to ensure the anticipated outcome. There were several instances in which the president and those within his inner circle simply failed in their attempt to convince the allies of the need for a military incursion. This was never more prevalent than in the infamous reference made in the State of the Union address as to the trafficking of nuclear materials through Niger when those claims were at that point only allegations by Ambassador Joseph Wilson, and not proven fact. He then continued to set forth an agenda even after the plan had been vetoed by major players in the UN circle. This inability to discuss and find a compromise with the allies remains the greatest mistake throughout Bush's terms, as it not only is a major reason for the allies' current position, but also broke the ties that in may ways bind the organization as a whole, in its mandate to provide security and stability throughout the globe.

As the premise of this chapter is to distribute blame, with the goal of extracting positive action from prior misjudgments, it is therefore imperative that the president and his cabinet acknowledge the central idea with regard to the allies.

The allies are your right hand! They are your eyes and ears around the globe. And yet the US has alienated many of its closest supporters, and in various cases that very support has led to the defeat of governments, purely due to the sympathetic response from their heads of state.

Within the last three years, the curtains have fallen on key supporters, from ex–British prime minister Tony Blair to ex–Italian prime minister Silvio Berlusconi. The sheer volatility of an alliance with the current US government regarding Iraq is POLITICAL SUICIDE! Where does this leave the US with respect to foreign relations, financial support, and troop levels?

Over the past years, the US government has become a desolate island, distanced from mainstream thought and draped in the haze as though its very existence had no bearing on future events. It has now become a government in which the entire supporting cast around the world is simply waiting for the revolving door to open and close over the current administration.

Despite the negativity, this government can do its part in rewriting future history, as opposed to people writing it for them. But in order for this to happen, the US has to ask itself some tough questions, the answers to which will provide true results and, more importantly, the light required to find its way through the dark tunnels it has carved. Note that each of these questions must be answered to the best of America's ability, to create the energy and belief that the war can still be won. These include key alliances that must be forged with those whose help is desperately needed, such as the French and the Russians. So what must the US offer to its allies on the bargaining table? How does the administration go about presenting the urgency of the situation, from its need for foreign troop numbers to ensure stability in the war zone to its need for financial assistance from the UN?

More importantly how does one overcome the current inertia associated with the given situation, or all of the ill feeling garnered to date between the governments and their respective leaders? Simple: a quick and honest phone call to each of the key allies, in which President Bush extends an olive branch. It is a simple gesture and yet one that speaks volumes; if and only if it is authentic. In the end, it is the president's job, nay, his DUTY, to put the welfare of his country and its people before his pride and the pride of his party, and act in the manner befitting the sacrifices made by all those who came before him.

After all, it is in service to others that we serve ourselves and the greater cause. It is this spirit, this resolve, that will transcend and crush all differences in opinion that currently exist.

To begin, the allies would have to include those key members of the UN Security Council with voting privileges, in particular those nations that voted against the resolution for war back in 2003 prior to the start of the engagement.

In particular the US would have to turn to its old friends and key allies and provide the necessary concessions to sway the tide toward a mutual consensus on progress in Iraq. Recall that it was the French themselves who expressed their refusal against "any" resolution for war in Iraq that would have been set forth by Secretary Powell at the UN. Winning French support and the key French vote is a crucial step in the acquisition of support from other key allies that would quickly follow their lead. Further to this climactic shift, other key players in the EU will follow suit, including crucial help from Germany, as well as the return and reinforcement of Italian and Spanish troops.

One of the other key players is undoubtedly the Russian Republic. Its vote is also a crucial one, yet recent US-Russian relations have been frigid at best. Here lies an opportunity to work together and build a friendship that will in its own right secure the safety of two peoples. On many occasions, only when one is forced to work with others does one realize the benefits of the eventual friendship that results. In this case, as the situation is extremely delicate in nature, only trusted representatives are to be tasked with communication duties such that no further conflicts result from the discussions.

Further friendships must be called upon, such as those with Australia and particularly Canada as its neighbor to the north could muster a great deal of political backing on the US's behalf, if its government so chooses.

In addition, the US must look to its Asian allies such as China, South Korea, Malaysia, etc., without emitting any shockwaves throughout the region, as issues already exist regarding the checkpoint with North Korea. The idea is to divide US needs for resources, manpower, financing, etc. amongst many, thereby reducing the quantity that each would require to supply to the overall effort.

If such a situation were to occur, the US would undoubtedly have to remain the overall force, supplying 50% of the total cost and manpower. The other resources would come from all the allies mentioned above, namely 10% from France, the UK, and Russia, respectively, then an additional 5% from Italy, Spain, Australia, and Canada, and the remaining 10% from all other remaining countries. The troop level of about 200,000 would constitute a solid force and one that would unquestionably tip the balance in favor of the allies, without overtaxing them either. Careful attention must be paid to the logistics of the respective forces, as one would dread an outcome in which Iraq or even Baghdad might be split along a tangible line, as was the case with Berlin subsequent to World War II. The intention would be to have mixed forces, or at least a rotation until the aftershocks subside and the Iraqi people control their own fate. In actuality, the grander question concerns how US emissaries will convince the allies that such actions are in their best interests and are the only solution to the current situation.

The answer itself is quite simple: one must share the wealth amongst friends, especially when those friends were present during trying times. Iraq's wealth, apart from its place in history as the site of ancient Babylon, lies beneath the surface. It is this precious commodity that will save its people, as it can be used as the way to repay all those who have helped. As such, one must ensure that each of the governments, according to their respective representation in the conflict, will be allocated a particular concession, such as reduced rates on fuel imports for x number of years.

Furthermore, oil revenues would need to be pooled into special accounts that would purposely render higher-than-normal returns. It is these funds that will ultimately rebuild the infrastructure and reduce the cost to each nation involved.

Even more importantly, it would allow Iraq to pay for its own construction. In addition, the countries that provided support during the campaign would then establish a semipermanent base in order to provide aid to the maturing Iraqi army/police. This may appear to be a full-scale colonization/occupation, but such forces will only stay to guard the country alongside their Iraqi counterparts. This in many regards appears to be a huge task with little reward, but one must realize that it would provide the stability required for many of the Iraqis around the world to return to their country, and help their adoptive country at the same time. It would further provide a direct link to the Arabic culture and a greater understanding of the people, as new communities would be born throughout the countryside.

Also, each company that so chooses will have the right to set up sites with drastically reduced income tax rates to promote commerce and trade on all fronts, not just the oil trade. Such rates would be in effect for 5 to 10 years such that the company could really benefit from the savings, and more importantly the average Iraqi citizen would truly profit, as they would then have the opportunity for a steady income. That effect alone would cause such a shockwave throughout even the tiniest of communities.

The last note is of historical importance, as those countries that participate will have the chance to be founding members of a powerful coalition that brought prosperity and freedom to a country and a people in need! The benefit to them may appear elusive, but in actuality it would bring more peace and an unquestionable ally strategically located in the Middle East.

In order to create the fiasco that currently exists, there were undoubtedly many other characters involved in laying down the blueprints for war. It is by careful analysis of these plans that the majority of the participants will begin to enter the field of vision, thereby allowing the government the opportunity to reprimand those that acted against the well-being of the republic and ensuring that such actions will not be repeated in the future—at least in the near future anyway. As oil remains one of the founding reasons for war, there is an unquestionable link between powerful companies and occupied position via the ever-prominent and powerful Washington lobbyists. Before continuing any further, I would like to add that lobbyists are by no means "detrimental to society," but there seems to be a great deal of evidence to the contrary, as they have often mingled in government affairs, thereby delaying and sometimes altering the expected decision. One could argue that by blaming the lobbyists, one is basically blaming an industry and thus the key players in that industry, and in many ways this is the case; but by pursuing this option, the government can still attack the problem and therefore the industry without getting its hands too dirty or dragging a particular company through the mud, as the government would be blaming entities indirectly via different lobbyist groups. The ability to neutralize the threat coming from a particular industry seems to be an insurmountable task. How does one thus create a positive change to this well-known Washington loophole within the confines of a chosen end and the means required to obtain the desired outcome? The best way is to use the power of the government to back the will of the people and let the government give to the people what they have forcibly cried out for. Regardless of the industry, it is again, as at any time throughout history, a time for an individual to truly envision and therefore overcome the inertia associated with the above-mentioned actions. In this case the war is heavily dependent on America's need for a constant oil supply.

It is therefore the government's duty to protect its people by using a roundabout response. This government, or the new government, will sacrifice by exiting Iraq and thereby give up a substantial percentage of the available and lucrative oil supply. This will in turn cause a significant increase in the cost of gas, which will enrage business and cause the economy to fall. In response the lobbyists will ask Congress to stay in Iraq and continue the fight, but the people will respond by choosing a president and a party that will obey their wishes. Then, having exited Iraq, a large portion of the budget will be used for other projects, one of which will be an environmental revolution that will give rise to two or three technologies that can be mass produced. Throughout this time, oil lobbyists will do everything in their power to sabotage this monumental project, and it will be up to the president-elect and his party to keep the project's heart beating, until the people, the organizations, and the "machine" of public opinion will force the public and scientific community to put the idea into reality. There will be a point in time at which the oil industry and the lobbyists will not be able to stop the will of the people, and it will be at this point that they too will do whatever it takes to ensure that their industry will control and profit from the new technology, all the while reaping the final 10 to 15 years of gains from the "old" oil industry. This back-and-forth approach is a means by which the president and the American public will make use of each other and the opportunity presented to them despite US failure in Iraq. This crucial point in time would allow Washington and its allies to transform a losing situation into a chosen ending that will benefit not only the American people but the welfare of the ecosystem of our world as a whole for this and many generations to come; all the while giving those in power the ability to embark upon and profit from the opportunity that lies before them should they choose to take part in this master plan.

Obviously, this scenario has many players, including the president (both current and future), the political parties, the lobbyists, feedback from the economy, the response from the scientific community, the anticipated feedback from the enemy, and finally the will of the people and their ability to cause a revolution! In many ways this situation represents reality and the actions that can occur if the situation is handled delicately with trusted US government officials at the controls and as many allied nations as possible in the copilot's seat.

Another entity that has received much criticism from the very start of the "War on Terror" is the CIA and its top spy, Director George Tenet. The list of reasons for pinpointing the agency with blame for 9/11 as well as the war itself has been particularly harsh, as the view of Congress, the press, and the average American has been one of utter failure by the agency. The people have criticized with all fairness its ability to recover decisive intelligence prior to 9/11, that they should have acted upon the information they had and convinced President Bush and former president Clinton of the need to attack terrorist strongholds. The newspapers also noted the agency's lack of Arabic-speaking officers, translators, and resources, all necessary to even understand any information that might be intercepted. Perhaps the greatest criticism results from the television image implanted in many minds, in which then Secretary of State Colin Powell sat before the United Nations council, presenting the US case for war, with Director Tenet and FBI Director Mueller basically serving as the stamp of approval and trust for the message conveyed to the entire world. This in many ways is the most damaging of any point on the list, as war was declared soon after. Despite the fact that the CIA is to a certain degree at fault, as they were unable to uncover the master plans being laid out by Bin Laden's terrorist organization, the CIA was nevertheless aware, with many of their agents requesting and shouting out for action. One must recall that the agency deals with matters of national security on a daily basis; similarly to any other company in the corporate world, it was overwhelmed by the overload and in this case failed to prioritize and present the case for the capture of Bin Laden and his subordinates. This does not mean that the agency was not aware but was most probably unable to convince the president of the urgency at hand. Regardless of the reasoning, the premise of this chapter remains the ability to bring about change in order to create the future envisioned by the president, the government, and the people. In order to do so, and therefore bring concrete, positive change to the intelligence community so that it can do its jobs more efficiently, the agency must set forth a plan that will address each of these factors.

Given the volatility of the times, as the situation deteriorated, it was all too easy to simply fire the director in order to show that the government had done its part in assigning blame and finding a solution to the events that took place under Director Tenet's watch. In reality, the real goal is to set forth a program with filters that will allow the agency to efficiently compartmentalize incoming data, thereby allowing agents the opportunity to intervene at the optimal moment.

With respect to the CIA, regardless of the plans or the chosen end to the Iraq war, the organization as a whole will always require a greater budget, with which it can focus its effort on the nations of interest and the Middle East as a whole. This should therefore include the recruitment of American citizens of Arabic descent, preferably born in the US, such that both the name and the face would easily fit into a Middle Eastern setting. These agents would be set up in the Middle Eastern business world, thereby using familiarity and the trust factor to infiltrate and uncover suspicious activity. This would be supplemented by a drastic increase in translating capabilities, along with new software to sift through the "chatter heard" both over the telephone lines as well as via the Internet. What one must not forget is that the agency, despite its central role in the

Arabic world, must monitor and act on any and all threats throughout the globe. This includes threats from North Korea, current disagreements with Russia and China, oil threats from South American nations such as Venezuela, and the numerous conflicts throughout Africa. As such, the director must ensure that despite the heavier distribution of resources centered in the Middle East, it must not lose focus of the numerous other enemies strategically situated throughout the globe. Furthermore, despite the effort made to group all the agencies under a single umbrella, there appears to be an unbreakable barrier between the CIA and the FBI on matters of national security. This culture of the FBI for internal threats versus the CIA for external threats can no longer continue to exist, as their goals are both aimed at national security. This does not mean that all files on the Iraqi conflict should be shared between the two agencies, but there should be a group or software program or a mix of the two, the sole purpose of which is to verify, evaluate, and distribute those files that may be of use to both or either agencies; and that would be a separate organization if need be; regardless, it must be objective. This group would of course be completely dependent on the information provided by both organizations, as it could very well result in a "garbage in–garbage out" scenario should both organizations fail to be forthcoming with regard to current projects.

From the public's point of view, the CIA must provide the intelligence it can, whether the US chooses the exit strategy or not in Iraq. Regardless, the bigger question with this variable thus remains the secrecy behind their work and the inability of the public to monitor its progress. This is one of those strange cases where silence and the lack of any catastrophic events may provide comfort to the American people that the agency is doing everything in its power to protect them from those who would harm the homeland. In many ways, the most efficient strategy would be one in which the people force the government to provide the agency with a greater budget, with proper checks and balances set in place, of course, all the while providing a certain recognition of the work done by some of the most loyal individuals who have sacrificed their lives for their country. This in no way suggests that the media divulge the work in progress, but perhaps provide a glimpse at past efforts that paid dividends despite having gone completely unnoticed by the public at large. In many ways, this simply would provide confirmation to those individuals that their work is paramount to national security, and thus remind them of the incredible day-to-day work they do. This of course assumes that the media does not repeat the blunder that occurred with Ambassador Joseph Wilson and his CIA undercover wife.

One could also channel the blame onto the commission set up purposely to critique and possibly veto the decisions set forth by the Bush administration subsequent to 9/11. It was understood by all those who partook in the discussions that the heated debates would almost certainly lead to offensive retaliatory efforts somewhere in the world, and it was up to these representatives, both Democrat and Republican, to ensure American interests. It was during these discussions that key nominees such as Senator Clinton, Senator Kerry, and others gave support to the president with nearly carte blanche powers so that he could have the support to carry out the difficult decisions on the horizon.

What they failed to remember was that it was precisely at that time that they, as members of the commission, could have both demonstrated their courage under political fire and their patriotism to the country. These individuals, especially Democrats, could have included key clauses that would have limited the president's power, thereby limiting his ability to initiate certain actions without requiring the commission's approval. One could argue that the Democrats simply followed the Republican lead and that in many ways they dodged the pressure associated with America's "need" to respond to terrorist threats, thus leaving their party in a mode based purely on criticism, as opposed to finding viable solutions for the decision that followed. Conversely, throughout the last year, whether the exit strategy proves to be the proper course of action or not, at least the Democrats set forth a concrete plan and have chosen to accept the losses. As the commission itself contains a number of key members whose credibility may be compromised given their change of opinions from their initial position, one might consider recycling the faces within the discussion room in the hope that this may provide a breath of fresh air and perhaps a renewed partnership between the new members of both parties. More importantly it may even provide hope for the people paying attention to any recommendations that might be made by the group. Furthermore, one must recall that the Armed Services Committee contains certain key Democrats, such as Senator Clinton and Senator Biden, who in may ways were already in a position to direct US policy in the direction of their party's values. They, in many ways, could have opposed or at least interfered with the proposed plans but instead provided the go-ahead as the president requested. At this stage in the game, the committee should choose to unite under a common goal so that however short of the original plans, their anticipated outcome will come into being.

There are also those that have questioned the position of the allies concerning the state of US influence or the lack thereof, which will undoubtedly cause turmoil that will reach their respective shores. If one were to backtrack to either the start of the conflict or even perhaps the six-month or one-year mark of the war, the weight of allied forces would have most certainly tipped the scale in the favor of the US and the UN as a whole.

It is quite possible that after English, Italian, and Spanish aid was sent to the region, had the French, Germans, and Russians agreed, Iraq could very well have been the light of the Middle East. A democratic jewel in so-called "dark quarters." This in no way suggests that the democratic idea is just a Western idea and the Arabic idea is flawed, it only points to the fact that for the first time Western democracy would have been implanted into the heart of the Middle East. All one has to do is consider the battle for Kuwait that took place during President Bush's mandate in which the entire UN stood united and there was no limit to their possibilities. Obviously, we cannot go back in time and undo America's mistake in its inability to convince the allies, but there is some weight to this argument despite my personal disagreement with the factor as a whole. The important fact, in many ways the moral of the story, remains that for all future conflicts, including certain key disagreements with countries like North Korea and Iran, no action should be taken unless the majority of the key UN members agree. In the case of the proposed US exit strategy, it is now the UN's turn to provide logistical help, including military support, to ensure that the operation goes through with minimal loss of life and interference with the US plans. At this point, it would be in the interest of the UN to have troops on the ground that would serve a dual purpose: firstly to help the US with its exit, as explained above, and thereby end the feud between allies; and secondly to show the world that the UN still has weight and will continue to serve all the nations in the best interests of peace and stability.

In many ways there is still one last entity to which blame is to be assigned. It is obvious that the president is given a mandate by the people who agree with his ideas and support the actions taken. Back in 2000, when President Bush first came into office, the people voted in an election that split the country in two distinct halves, either Democrat or Republican, as had never been seen in American history. Regardless, the people's decision was in many ways of no consequence, as the attack on 9/11 came a few months after. The problem remains the 2004 election, in which the people were clearly told by the president of the plans to stay the course in Iraq. There was no attempt at hiding these plans or even talk of a specific timeline that would be respected to end the conflict; and despite the uncertainty, the American people clearly spoke and gave the president a second mandate and ultimately four more years of war. When one examines this crucial moment in time and its effect on the present and future, one cannot help but assign blame to the people as well. Obviously Democratic voters will automatically scream out in opposition that they disagreed, but one of the pitfalls of democracy remains the simple fact that the majority rules—this now becomes the people's turn to give the government their new mandate for their future with the upcoming election in November of 2008. Again, despite eight years of Republican views, the American people have to choose the "candidate," and not the party, at this crucial junction in time who will direct the nation according to their wishes while being strong and persuasive enough to ensure America's standing for decades to come. Regardless, subsequent to that crucial November evening in 2008, people will have no excuse if their chosen representatives do not act accordingly.

In closing, this chapter served in many ways as a place in which one could exhale and basically single out and blame those who were directly and indirectly responsible for the current situation in Iraq. Despite doing so, and feeling better afterward, the goal remains the proposal and implementation of ideas that will produce the expected outcome, thereby maintaining America's control over the war, its direction, and the global situation. As such, every face on the dart board was supplemented with suggestions that may produce the "chosen end." It is now up to the people to push forward their agenda and the government to listen, understand, and implement the will of the people. In many ways, we now have to stand back and watch the show.

# CHAPTER 3

# The Right Party for the Job

THERE IS NO RIGHT party for this monumental task; there are only "right minds"—those individuals in government who are not looking out for number one; those individuals who actually have the best interest of the troops and the Iraqi people at heart and ironically the best interest of the enemy as well.

This does not mean that the government must aid the enemy but understand what fuels them. What actually made them despise America to such a degree and how can those issues be resolved, thus disarming them and their link to the people? To top it all off, within this tangled web is an election for office in which all sides claim to have the answers.

As the situation has steadily progressed in the negative direction, rhetoric from Washington has steadily increased in nature, content, and severity. Ultimately, if one ponders the stance of both parties, one asks whether they are really that different and whether any of the two actually want victory in Iraq. After all, victory is a loose term used in Washington these days, whose degree varies immensely depending on the crowd.

In actuality, the 2008 platform exists of two parties that have accepted defeat, with the Democratic view being one of rapid retreat, and the Republican view a slow-paced version of the former. As is the case, the US will lose and the only choice is whether to lose quickly or slowly! Is that the choice Americans want to make? Note that for the time being, ignore all other major issues, from immigration policies to health care reform, and simply focus on the immense, baron plateau that is Iraq!

As it stands today, amongst all the haze, who is the one candidate that really stands out or at least provides hope for the future in all regards, both from the standpoint of Iraq as well as other domestic and foreign policies? Who is the one person that steps across party lines and appeals to both points of view? As the field of candidates is immense, the choice appears to be endless, just as the number of pulpits during each debate appears to form an endless arc. It is among the two political parties that one candidate in particular appears to possess all of these qualities and the tested ability to use them accordingly. Throughout this person's term in office, he or she has dealt with human tragedy, crime, budgets, manpower issues, and the media. This individual has demonstrated the abilities required of a leader and will do so when sworn into office. Lastly, this individual's response contains the right mix of all the attributes required from a head of state—and not just any head of state, but the office of the president of the United States.

Before divulging the individual's name, history has shown that the best of leaders have been those that absolutely felt as though the office were their destiny and that no other could provide the direction for the country that they could. All of the greatest leaders, from Caesar to Napoleon to Kennedy, felt that calling, as political office is a place where the community, including the international community, can be changed with the stroke of a pen.

With regards to the Democrats, I believe that there really is little or no strategy whatsoever regarding Iraq. They have simply expressed their intent to pull out the troops, thus ensuring victory for the enemy. One after the other, they address their constituents and stomp on the Republicans and rightfully so, as the cause of the war revolves around the current White House staff, despite all the changing faces within the last year or so. Regardless, the people should have at the very least a glimmer of hope with regard to their choice for office—that that person be the one person who can find the middle ground, better yet an actual position, under the cover of middle ground. Then a "true" diplomat would have been sworn into office.

So when one sifts through the candidates, the only candidates from the Democratic standpoint who appear to have diplomatic views are Senator Edwards and Senator Obama. Both of these candidates have not been in Washington for too long and therefore will not be held down significantly by the politics that preceded the act for war. Furthermore, they are both younger candidates with forward-looking agendas and fewer ties to the past. Whereas a candidate such as Senator Clinton, whose experience is draped in poor decision with respect to the war, is firmly planted in the past. At times it appears as though Bill were once again running for office and that on Election Day people may accidentally be voting for Bill instead of Hillary. Regardless of the Bill Clinton factor, and in particular with respect to Iraq, she has not persuaded the people to her side despite the campaign juggernaut that is thrusting her forward. One must recall that the other two candidates, as is the case for the rest of the bunch, do not have the same backing and yet they are at par with her, despite what the polls would have people believe. In essence, the majority of Americans would be more inclined to vote for Barack Obama or John Edwards, who have worked their way to the top, than a candidate who has had an opportunity at everything. Never underestimate the "rising from the ashes" factor that both Senators Obama and Edwards have going for them and the irresistible appeal of their union on the Democratic ticket. Lastly, Americans want a White House that is truly a family-oriented household, in spite of the overwhelming duties entrusted to the president. Here again, the values of both Obama and Edwards will shine through, as the authenticity appears to be genuine in nature. Regardless, as I wrote earlier, there is one candidate who still stands out amongst the others, and as you might have guessed, it is a Republican. Note that I am not a Republican or a Democrat, as I am truly a third-party participant, but just for the record, I believed that John Kerry was the man for the job during the 2004 race, but the American people thought differently. I have also been a true admirer of Kennedy as well as Reagan, and I will always try to orient myself toward the "Right Choice," the "true north."

It is in that regard that Rudy Giuliani stands out amongst all candidates either Democrate or Republican. He is the only candidate that can be "mistaken" to be a member of either party with respect to certain issues such as abortion, where he appears to belong on the other side of the aisle. It is what one would refer to as his "chameleon" factor, appealing to all the American people as he pursued the American dream in full—a son of immigrants, who brought New York City back to its pinnacle and was present in mind, body, and spirit for the people and the city when it needed him most. He is the only candidate that has shown his abilities long before any talk of primaries or presidential races.

Furthermore, Giuliani brings to the Republican party the element it lacks most: the ability to attract big city voters. Those who tend to vote Democrat. When one analyzes the situation, he appears to possess a fundamental characteristic: he is not a rigid present-day Republican, who tends to alienate voters from the party. Instead he comes across as a leader who is a member of the party of Lincoln. The future leader of a country and party that truly stands for all the people and his tenure in New York City was just that. Furthermore, his stance on crime as the U.S. attorney for the Southern District of New York showed his ability to confront the criminal element, thereby displaying another element lacking in differing degrees by all the other candidates on both sides of the aisle.

He is also passing through similar circumstances as former French president Jacques Chirac, who was the mayor of Paris prior to his entrance at Les Champs Elysée. Apart from all this talk is a man who climbed and will climb the ultimate ladder in the political world—a leader that will be able to extend the olive branch to his European allies and mend the relationships that currently exist, although he must be extremely vigilant during these trying times, as he is of Italian descent and is Catholic and as such must observe and react to the forces within his own party, as sabotage and treachery may be lurking in the corridors. These very differences, along with his magnetic style, will in many ways create friction amongst his peers. In the end one must realize that the party is irrelevant because what the people really vote for is the person, and those candidates who do prevail, at least prior to 2000, were the candidates that made opposing party believers sympathetic and want to vote for the "enemy." Regardless, the new president, come 2008, or vice president depending on the rising stardom of Senator McCain, will once again hail from the great state of New York.

To recap, it is obvious that in politics, fact provides the reason for being, but emotion fuels the fire that hurls one past the finish line. The right party for the job is therefore the one whose chosen candidate can provide to both sides of the aisle that form of activism and bipartisanship that represents not only the US government but the American people as a whole. Regardless, in the context of taking the relevant steps toward a chosen end, one must endure all the criticism and venom from one's peers.

That candidate must at times be as clear as the water flowing through a pristine river and then at times as murky and opaque as the water at the depths of a deep, dark ocean. In so keeping, the candidate must have the cunning, cutthroat ability that is entrusted in them by the people. In many ways, it is somewhat like religious blind faith, that this person will create the intended outcome, all the while allowing for tolerance despite the added constraint of a limited timeframe. As emotion will most certainly prevail over reason, the true candidate, the right candidate, and therefore the right party, will be he or she who in many ways shows his/her cards at the optimal time in this expensive and treacherous game. That candidate must be ready to explain a real plan to the American people consisting of a so-called exit strategy, an elongated version of that idea or otherwise as well as the adjoining timetable for the completion of the chosen objective. Of course, that plan can be tweaked as need be and as the situation dictates, but it will demonstrate that this particular candidate is willing to show his/her hand to the people in the hopes of being entrusted with the completion of the mission. This step is critical, as it will put all his or her words from then to the present into context and ultimately provide the necessary steps to bring those ideas into reality.

One could argue that any foolish politician can easily do so, and thereby provide the enemy with plans with which to counterattack American initiatives associated with the chosen ending. This opinion is entirely justified and maintains its balance via the future president's ability to both force and gently persuade those around him/her toward the end result. Then should the president decide to do otherwise after taking office, it would be his/her decision and yet completely plausible as commander-in-chief to choose wisely and in the best interests of the country's welfare.

Regardless, if history has taught us anything, it would be the very fact that it often repeats itself. If this were to take place, a Republican win could further lead to continued conflict in Iraq or elsewhere, whereas a Democratic win could possibly lead to bureaucratic idling around the demanding decisions that require the consensus of numerous councils. Despite the endless pros over this decision of the right party for the job and its ability to set forth the proper agenda toward the chosen end, the arguments stated were done so to demonstrate that proper actions are not set forth by the party but rather by the individual who provides the vision. The party simply helps pave the way to bring those ideas into existence. Basically voters must choose the person and that person's ideas, passion for the proper course of action, and abilities to make it happen. The party simply shows its support and comes along for the ride.

# CHAPTER 4

# *Positioning in the Middle East*

IF ONE WERE TO look at Iraq's position on a world map, one would quickly realize its prime location in the region. One might even call it the "heartland of the Middle East," although some may wholeheartedly despise that analogy altogether. Regardless, the American people and US allies, whether these governments see themselves that way or not, must realize the numerous possibilities/opportunities available should the region become democratized, thus allowing open and free commerce.

This return, what I refer to as the "rebirth of Babylon," would provide tremendous returns for the entire global community but most importantly a wealthy, peaceful future for the Iraqi people, a well-deserved change from their current reality.

From an Iraqi standpoint, the infusion of company sites, historical research, and IT investments will give the people the opportunity and stability that they have long desired. They would finally have the ability to earn a steady income, thus allowing the people, their families, and therefore the country to prosper and move forward.

Furthermore, Iraq's location will provide close proximity to potential US enemies, thus providing the capabilities to rapidly organize the logistics for any military incursion or battle that might arise on a moment's notice or that may be simmering over the years. Such preparations could include key airports along its borders, including intelligence offices that could be set up with Iraqi personnel leading the investigations after a brief period of CIA and foreign intelligence instruction. This very capability would provide invaluable information for the security of both Iraq and the allies. After all, one must be intimate with the enemy to monitor their movements, and here is that perfect opportunity to do both, for national and international security for all peoples around the world.

In addition, from the point of view of oil refining, guarded installations would allow the international community access to a steady surplus of oil all year round, with Kuwait now an ally providing the simplest access route to transport. As allies, Iraqis would look to their Kuwaiti neighbors as a route to the Persian Gulf and transport via the Indian Ocean to clients worldwide, once invaders, now both friends and business partners. Better still, via their newfound friendship, under the newly democratized republic, a route could also be established via Jordan with final access to the Mediterranean via Lebanon or Israel. If the resources permit, both plans of action could be implemented, thereby insuring the dissemination of the precious cargo.

In relation to the information above, a consortium of US sympathizers could be established that would cut off links between Iran and Syria. The consortium along a "north-south line" consisting of friendly nations would extend from Turkey to Iraq along its northern border with its central portion consisting of Iraq/Jordan/Israel, with the imaginary access continuing its course through Kuwait and Saudi Arabia. This "north-south line" would in essence create a powerful organization with countries that would neutralize the threat from within simply due to the positioning of pieces across a living, breathing chess board. Also, if allied troops, including Canadian, could diminish threats in Afghanistan to acceptable levels along with continued support from Pakistan, this would have a compressive effect on Iran. It would not fully control the area, but that is not the goal. The true goal within the region is to establish friendships by providing the people the essentials, the most important of which is security, which will in time, synthesize into a healty economy and prosperity for the Iraqi people and the region as a whole.

Lastly, the psychological effect of Iraq's position in the Middle East may be the point of greatest interest, as it affects the manner in which the country acts and the forcefulness of its actions. If one considers past campaigns, form Napoleon's conquest of Egypt to Caesar's hold over the Rubicon, the act of gaining or protecting the land in question is one of prime psychological importance. It implants the possibility of the envisioned end result and provides the endorphins that nourish the will to succeed. In this case, the US and its allies, if they were to choose victory over defeat in Iraq, will have secured a centralized territory within a complicated landscape upon which the goal, the true master plan, can be founded—one that would include a central location, a central flame, to add to the numerous other flames within the area. In many ways, Iraq constitutes a psychological and physical showdown in which opposing forces collide, and for the aftermath will constitute a haunting reminder for the loser. A victory would lend itself to the slideshow of history, including images of the overtaking of a communist regime, to the tumultuous years of rebellion, to a center of freedom with the confines of a closed community.

All this can still be if the government thinks in this manner and makes the changes accordingly as the military brass suggests. What the president must do, despite his lame duck status, is drive home the idea of victory by explaining what victory means in the context of positioning, the central role it will play in the national security of Iraq, and the friendships that could be founded and forged with bordering states as Iraq would mature into a true model democracy.

What Iraq's location has done for the people may be considered both a burden and a blessing, as its position has provided the country and its population the opputunity to reinvent itself as it sees fit and establish itself as a central hub through which Middle Eastern conflicts can be appropriately addressed. On the other hand, a loss, which appears to be the end result should the current situation remain unchanged, would result in a catastrophic outcome, as Iraq would then provide a crucial artery through which trafficking of all types could openly take place. Furthermore, its numerous inputs resulting from bordering on a few questionable states, will create a magnetic effect in which all terrorist activities would be immediately and forcefully attracted.

# CHAPTER 5

# The Hearts and Minds of Iraqis

ONE OF THE CENTRAL goals of this war, or any war, if one is to truly claim victory for one's actions, remains the all-important sentiment of the people; what has come to be known as the "hearts and minds" of the people.

In past conflicts such as World War II, the people in many ways were much the same as their conquerors and very similar to their liberators. When US forces liberated the French, or Canadian forces liberated the Dutch, the liberator and those freed from the grips of the conqueror may have spoken different languages, but the two parties had a great deal in common, from the democracies in place to the religion they practiced.

Given the new setting in the Middle East, which in many ways is really an old one, when one backtracks through history, one quickly realizes that there are actually two fronts to contend with if the US and its allies are to truly win the hearts and minds of the people. The first is undoubtedly religion, and the other is the knowledge and understanding that the allies are not invaders. As to whether allied plans are to invade or not is not even important; what is paramount is the Arabic perception of the situation.

When it comes to religion, there is a notion of the impossibility of reaching any kind of agreement, as the idea of Christians invading Muslim territories goes back to the time of the Crusades. What a government must do is not deny the majority Christian faith of the allied armed forces, as that will only aggravate the Arabic nations both in Iraq and around the world, but simply to make that issue background information. Presently, to American eyes, that fact was easily accomplished, but I believe that the situation is very different in the region, as talk in Washington is not confined to the White House, the House, or the Senate.

Regardless of the discussions concerning invasion and/or religion, there are irrefutable messages that can be sent to the Iraqi/Arabic population that are undeniable, and will undoubtedly make their way to the very heart of the individual.

Some changes in particular are very concrete and must be implemented immediately in order to allow the appropriate lead time for the enhancement of the aftershock.

First and foremost, America and its allies must begin to rebuild the Iraqi infrastructure, and they must do so NOW! This action will speak volumes to the Iraqis because it will affect them immediately and will provide the psychological high needed to take them over till the point at which the project comes into being. Such projects would include water and drainage facilities, coupled with proper plumbing and hydroelectric facilities to power their homes and businesses. This will be a tremendous investment but one that could be paid based on the country's rich oil deposits. Iraq would leverage its future on its most requested resource, oil.

In addition, certain ideas that are common knowledge in the US can be implemented in Iraq as well. Take Habitat for Humanity as an example. The idea of having people build their own houses with the help of the US Army Corps of Engineers will provide divdends on both fronts, from the usage of people in the city occupying their time working as opposed to time spent within groups preaching the terrorist movement, not to mention the direct one-on-one relationship that would be forged between the army engineers/soldiers and the people. Working together to build a house will transform itself into an indestructable link between the people and the allies.

In addition to providing shelter, the allies must ensure the food supply, and the best way to do so is to help the people solve their agricultural problems so that they can help themselves, thereby creating a self-sustaining society. Here again, army specialists or contract specialists would supply the expertise required to ensure that they are properly informed. Perhaps even make it such that the same soldier goes to speak with the same people so that the US-Iraq tie becomes a personal one with a face, as opposed to government aid.

Lastly, the allies must rally all the medical community throughout Iraq to ensure that both American and allied doctors are working side by side with their Iraqi counterparts to ensure the welfare of the people. This will demonstrate to the Iraqi people the compassion of the West and will touch the people one family at a time. Furthermore, the opening of old hospital sites within the region would invigorate the people, as it would provide not only physical care, but also the psychological boost needed—the people would feel that help is there, should any be required; and given the times in Iraq, it is definitely needed.

Now that the main points are addressed, namely food, shelter, and medical attention, it would be with the next few points that the allies could truly win over the people!

Despite the fact that a war is going on, the mind of the individual must be freed as much as possible in order to ensure sanity throughout the process that will lead to democracy or at least a form pertinent to the Iraqi society. The best way to do so, while winning over the people, is to provide entertainment in one form or another. Even during the Roman Empire, when a Roman city was built, one of the central structures of the city was its center for games, i.e., a mini-coliseum. This will distract the people and allow the mind to breathe and enjoy itself. As such, the army engineers/architects should pick out a site or a few sites if possible on which to build an arena for a few thousand people (or even one for a few hundred to start) that is logistically viable from a security standpoint. This venue would be apart from the markets so that it is truly a place to let go and free the mind. Furthermore, it must serve as a place that is free of the current politics and is centered on and around the games. A perfect example would be a soccer pitch, in which local teams could take part to rally the people and show that competition between the factions is perfectly healthy, but unification and solidarity is the goal. Also, this same pitch could serve as a place to hold bazaars and celebrate festivals, religious events, and others as a community. The bazaars could include food-tasting days, where people are to cook dishes so that all can come and taste the other tribe's cuisines. In such cases, allied soldiers would add their food to the mix, such as Italian dishes from Italian bases in Al Nasarya, to fish and chips from the British, to hamburgers from US forces, all with halal meat, of course. After all, there is no doubt that the way to a person's heart is through his stomach. Regardless of the form of entertainment chosen for the games, allied soldiers must take part so that Iraqis come to realize that the soldiers have a human side, as they do. Just picture it, a soccer match between Italian soldiers and Iraqi infantry or a baseball game between US soldiers and Iraqis. Wouldn't that be something!

Extending the olive branch does not stop there. The emotional/ personal side of this complicated relationship must be nurtured as well. Fortunately there are many little actions that will create enormous reactions from the people at large. This idea is based on two simple notions: firstly one is to treat the people like human beings just as though one were back home interacting with a neighbor, and secondly one should find commonalities and capitalize on them. Once again, these actions can be taken immediately—such as an impromptu supper with Iraqis with whom they normally speak with during their daily visits. It does not have to be a feast, but a simple sit down to eat something together. That interaction is personal, warming, and unforgettable, and it will become a habit after the first few times. Undoubtedly, the word would find its way to the ears of the Iraqi people. This same action could then have a second use, in which allied soldiers could ask the Iraqis to show them Iraqi cuisine or ask about their history and family lineage, or artifacts they may have been producing throughout their families' histories. Whatever the case, it will be yet another chance to open up conversation between the allies and the people.

Lastly, there must be a point in the conversation where the people are asked about their family's losses. There will undoubtedly be anger toward US soldiers, but expressing the feelings with soldiers explaining their side will hopefully bring some kind of closure to the situation. This would be the optimal place to explain that those losses would not have been in vain if future generations were to live in a democratic Iraq, in which mindless death would no longer occur.

In addition, given the situation, there must be countless orphans walking aimlessly throughout Baghdad and other cities throughout Iraq. The allies could and should create orphanages to take care of these children, who are otherwise lost in society and are undoubtedly easy targets for terrorists recruiting for future members within their ranks.

In spite of the logistical issues at hand, helping the children will in many ways infiltrate into the hearts of the people. There are few facts that are common regardless of the setting throughout the world, and the welfare of children transcends all communities and people.

Furthermore, help the people help themselves by providing the education required to excel in the global community. Why not start with a nontraditional two-way class in which there would be English courses for Iraqis wanting to learn the language followed by Iraqis then teaching Arabic to willing individuals from allied forces. The two interactions would be illuminating to all involved and would again create an intangible link between the people and the soldiers because they would be helping each other, instead of a solely one-sided situation. Those classes could then be followed by a course pertaining purely to the welfare of women within the community. It would include discussions on contraception, education for women regarding career opportunities, and acceptable behavior within the homes, including both verbal and physical abuse. This would open a conversation between female officers and the women of the communities. The officers would provide the initial push to overcome the tremendous inertia associated with the status quo of women within the society. This is a major point to address within the community and should be handled with extreme caution, as the backlash could be disastrous. Regardless, it must be handled as soon as possible, as in the end these mothers will instill in their children the ideas that will be the foundation for the rest of their lives, as those children are tomorrow's society.

In addition, promote higher learning! I believe that a single act can create an enthusiasm for learning that most young people are yearning for: reopen Baghdad University. This does not mean that the US must reopen a huge campus, which would be a logistical nightmare, but a small section must be made available to the public so that a feeling of society coming together begins to infiltrate the psychology of the people by osmosis. It would create an excitement that would overtake any wall that had formed over the years, and most importantly, it would provide the notion that a better life is possible if they study and help their community with the knowledge they have learned throughout their curricula.

Apart from education, these ideas must be presented to the public at large in manners that will appeal to the average person. The propaganda must be convincing, emotional, and factual to attract the people such that the battle for the mind is won without a shot being fired. In this case, I believe that such an important task must be outsourced to the proper individuals—and who better than a Hollywood agency that works on promotions all year round? Ask and pay specific agencies to complete a study of the situation and produce a final report including all the recommendations on the particular manner in which the information could be disseminated throughout the community and the country as a whole. Ask them to make the message personal and emotional and how best to get that information into the laps of the average Iraqi. Obviously, this would be a joint venture between the hired agencies and the communication branch of the armed forces—but why not give this idea a try and thereby exhaust yet another possibility toward the goal of success for the country and its people?

I believe that Hollywood could provide successful recommendations and could add to the cause in a way that will truly help the Iraqi people and in turn the US military and all its allies. Nevertheless, support in this manner would by all means be extremely helpful to the cause instead of some twenty-second commercial fluff with a known actor speaking out against the war. What the campaign requires is positive action, not another useless, futile reaction to the situation.

All the suggestions within this chapter, if implemented, will massage the situation such that the element of trust between the people and the soldiers produces a strong link, with the Iraqi parliament as its bridge. One must not forget that true success in Iraq will be achieved only when a government with the support of the people is in place and provides the essential services that will foster growth and prosperity. As this is the goal, the government must at all costs represent all the people fairly, and it is left to allied governments to oversee the current caucus as to their progress over the first few years subsequent to victory. In the interim, the anonymity of US involvement must be camouflaged to the nth degree but must remain the voice of reason when discussions deviate outside the acceptable tolerance.

This oversight will create the framework for future governments, and in many ways on this front the US has administered favorably. As such, the allies must continue to persuade the parties to converse on the issues, especially with respect to the explosive ones that cause a great deal of distress, with oil revenues being one of the greatest challenges.

As the "hearts and minds" of the people is a very intangible quality, establishing the all-important KPIs (Key Product Indicators), will be a very difficult task. Regardless, the implementation of the above suggestions, some of which are simple while others require a great deal of planning and determination, will provide the foundation for future government institutions. What one cannot ignore is that anything and everything is created via an idea and grows and solidifies on this basis. In order to have people believe, there must first be trust and belief in the central idea, and once such a notion is accepted, it can never be stopped. Just like any revolution throughout history, no government or group can stop the will of the people once the flame is ignited. I believe that these ideas might very well be the spark required for the initial flame.

# CHAPTER 6

# How to Win the War

THE GENIUS OF ALL plans is twofold, continually working in parallel such that at any instant the alternate can be pursued at a loss or gain depending on the situation. Plans should in essence provide the flexibility for any situation; but regardless, each of them must have an end goal decided upon at the very outset that such an option was considered.

In spite of all the chatter, the goal first envisioned was and should have always been victory in the War on Terror, but due to diverging agendas, that war transformed itself onto the Iraqi stage. That setting has now become the setting for victory, and a defeat there would translate into a defeat in the new global war on terrorism. So if one were to now stand back and ignore the parallel options available at this time or anytime during the conflict, and concentrate solely on victory by any means, there are certain actions and mindsets that must be undertaken. If these words and actions continue to diverge, then defeat in Iraq is inevitable. Thanks to certain members of Congress, that defeat came at the very start of the war, before a single shot was fired. Only those few with the courage to reject the war during the voting process truly have the right to scold the government for its actions, as all others are as guilty of the death toll as is the president.

Given the context, and regardless of who is to blame for the current status of the conflict, the war could still be won, to a certain degree; but it will be up to the new government to ensure that future actions "parallel" the thoughts and will of the White House.

Firstly and most importantly, if one looks back at successful campaigns such as World War II, despite the numerous losses at the start of the war, the people were bombarded with messages, short films, and propaganda all explaining to—dare I say brainwashing—the people about the need for action and above all victory for allied forces. The idea was rampant throughout the free world such that it made people feel that not only was it a duty, it was the destiny of entrusted democracies to return order and justice to a world that had suddenly gone awry. Victory, whether the allies knew it or not, would present itself simply because they knew that people had decided that no other option was acceptable.

Now turn the  page to the present day, and yet again propaganda remains the sharpest instrument in this delicate surgery, except, as opposed to World War II, the scalpel has now been turned against the doctor. In essence all the current media propaganda has been telling the people, and even worse, confirming to the military, that the war is already lost!—that in essence their sacrifice was in vain and that their only goal is simply not to get captured or killed in action so that they can return home and hold their head high. Who throughout history held their head high and felt proud for a defeat apart from those exceptional cases such as the stand of the 300 Spartans on a glorious mountaintop. Again, it must be repeated that this is not a military failure; it is a government failure, which knows not the difference between red and blue. As such, the first action to take, or should I say jump-start, on the long road to victory is the restoration of the propaganda machine. Make the people believe once again that victory is not only possible but inevitable and that a defeat in the region cannot be tolerated. Disseminate the idea from the smallest town to the greatest metropolis around the globe—on the radio, via the Internet, on posters at the movies, everywhere! Again the key here is to make the people envision victory, feel victory, and taste victory. Without this key element, defeat is inevitable, and in many ways the current climate is already one of defeat. A change of tone from the right people can change the course of progress and the end-product virtually overnight if the president and the government consciously decide to choose victory over defeat.

Secondly, despite the facts that tend to point toward a lack of justification for the war, the American people and the rest of the allies must consciously ignore this option, as it will resonate throughout the battlefield and literally manifest itself in allied causalities on the front lines. This notion in no way pardons or erases the deeds of the Bush government, which was unquestionably the catalyst in the entire affair and rightfully deserves the greatest portion of the blame, but one must recall that many of the "lynchers" came from the other side of the aisle. Regardless, the time for blame has lingered long enough and will have its time in the spotlight throughout the 2008 presidential campaign, but in the meanwhile it is the advancement of the cause and the welfare of the soldiers that must be considered. With this idea in mind, it is up to US and allied government officials to turn a losing cause to their advantage and redirect the bull's horns toward the enemy instead of toward representative blue or red shirts. Given the situation, the US must reach out to its allies and ask for their help given that a great deal of the brunt has already been borne by the US military and US taxpayers. It would be a heartfelt request for aid to strengthen the posts that already exist throughout the country, all the while foreshadowing the consequences of procrastination.

Again, talk without action serves no purpose whatsoever and therefore must be accompanied by undeniable actions that will lead to firm results in the field. The military could do so on several fronts, beginning with a mass disruption of supply lines to terrorists, including control over the food supply. This action is as old as warfare itself and has provided the prelude to many of the greatest battles. Success on this front will discourage the enemy, cause infighting, and result in costly errors on the enemy's part. The only way to do so is via intelligence, especially through local Iraqi insiders who would be trusted by local insurgent groups.

Given the vastness of the country, it can be divided into sections with phases to be continually achieved, thus enlarging the hold over the area. This strategy could be put into practice throughout Baghdad and its outskirts and then slowly employed in other major areas till the neighborhoods meshed throughout the entire country.

In addition to the above, with the help of foreign government troops, the country can be divided into sections that would be monitored by numerous NATO commanders representing each country. That commander would have the ability to employ the procedures that he sees fit to ensure security within that specific territory. If the US were to be successful in the recruitment of aid from foreign countries, each of the country members would instill a method that could be used as a template by the rest of the commanders if considered applicable, or perhaps be confined to each of the areas. This tactic would in no way cause a breakup of the present-day Iraq, but would actually force the allies to consider the alternate solutions set forth by each of the NATO commanders. In order to have successful recruitment, ensure that US forces will continue to occupy the most dangerous areas to allow other countries time to understand and become more acquainted with the dangers lurking everywhere.

Furthermore, a healthy army is an efficient one. It is thus imperative that the rotation of soldiers in and out of Iraq remain a priority. As the network of US forces is an extensive one, it would be in the best interests of the entire armed forces that worldwide rotations take place to ensure both the physical and psychological well-beings of all enlisted personnel. Obviously the military has considered and implemented a rotation, but what must change in order to achieve victory in the end is the rate. No soldier or group of soldiers should be in the war zone for more than nine months to a year maximum. As the war is in its sixth year, no individual should be asked for more than two tours of duty, with an intermission between the two sessions. One must recall that a sane infantry officer can build bridges; an unhealthy one will simply destroy all the framework left behind by his/her comrades. Again, if the US could muster up support from its allies, the burden could be shared by all. This crucial fact is repeated throughout the text, as it cannot be overstated and it remains the president's and the government's obligation toward eventual failure or success in Iraq. To date, the government has failed on virtually every front with respect to international aid. The government to come in 2008 must address this issue if the war is to continue. Lastly, the irony of the troop rotation factor remains the central notion of acceptance, as the faith and tenacity of the military personnel is and has always been a source of great pride. It is again the government officials that are creating problems—through their constant discussion they have taken an already difficult fact and made it an absolutely painful one, as these discussions are endless and tend to serve only the political aspirations of the respective officials.

From a military standpoint, it would be beneficial to plan a military sweep of the major posts throughout the country, with the goal of direct control over the situation in each of the respective locations. The idea would consist of a schedule for the accomplishment of the post in question that would be the catalyst (and the "gate"), that would be necessary for initiating the procedure for gate two. There would have to be a list of factors that would have to be achieved to consider capture of the post and its future success. In the meantime, all US/allied posts, already under control, will remain under the status quo. The key to this process is allied aid, but in a "secondary sense" it would ensure minimal losses to the allies. The procedure would employ US soldiers/marines to sweep the area over an x period of time, three months for example, followed by an allied presence to police the area over the interim. This strategy would allow the US military to take the offensive position only, while allocating the defensive one to its allies. In many ways, if one were to stand back as a third party, it is a business plan in which the parent company makes the wave and then outsources the maintenance to another company. Recall that usually all companies involved in such a business deal stand to profit from such a situation, if and only if the final product is delivered, of course. This kind of speculation does seem rather cold and distant from the heat and sweat of the battlefield, but it is this type of calculated and modulated approach that will allow the military to slowly but surely secure an ever-growing Iraqi territory and population.

One of the primary factors required for the initiation of war is the fact that if one were to take place due to impending action from the aggressing party, the final outcome must result in victory. In other words, a war is to be fought if and only if victory is to be achieved. The belief at the start of the war was one of victory, although it is now obvious, and has been for some time, that the proper plans had not been set in motion. As such, new plans have to be laid out to secure victory, as opposed to the unanimous call for defeat in the war zone by both political parties throughout Washington. If one could now step back at this very moment in time, one would realize that victory can still be achieved via the simplest tactic of all—the threat of force. One might ponder as to how this is any different from what is being done at the moment, and the answer is simple. The current game plan is a physical one—this one is psychological, in which the threat would result from backdoor conversations with the heads of one or more of the following: Russia, China, and the western European powers. It would call for the mobilization of several thousands of soldiers from each of these nations, which would converge on Iraq and ensure victory. The beauty of this idea is that without firing a single shot, victory can be achieved from intimidation and fear alone. One of the key factors in this lies with the media, which will spread the idea, the propaganda, and the fear throughout the world. This idea will serve as the catalyst accompanied by certain small actions that would signal a great shift to the enemy and force him to back down or face the consequences that would otherwise consume and destroy any capability the enemy may possess. The new war would be one of words and would be won on allied terms, always taking into account the possibility that a coordinated strike could be necessary. If one were to describe the scene throughout the major capitals of the world, if this idea were to be implemented, one would witness the level of verbal aggression rise slowly and steadily over the course of a year or two; again, accompanied by the strategic positioning of the respective naval fleets in the Persian Gulf, for example.

Imagine, much to the dismay of the enemy and subsequent to months and months of talk on Russian and Chinese radio, that Moscow is sending out a carrier to the Gulf simply to "monitor the situation," to be followed by the influx of Chinese soldiers to help train Iraqi soldiers on orders from Beijing. The waves this would cause throughout the region would be undeniable. Recall that this is intended as a threat and is in line with the idea of psychological warfare. The interesting part of the current situation is that representatives from both parties are currently using this very idea against themselves by simply campaigning relentlessly against any further action except those associated with failure. But it is their job, nay, their duty, as possible presidents in waiting to ensure victory and future success and prosperity by implementing winning strategies as opposed to exit strategies and demoralizing those who fought throughout the ordeal. If one recalls, or chooses to recall, US forces were stationed in Japan and Germany for an extended period to ensure that these countries and their governments would continue to act accordingly. Given the precedence, why would the outcome of Iraq be any different? If anything, it would constitute an even greater obstacle than Germany or Japan ever were, given the fact that those two countries were at least unified to begin with, as opposed to the three-way segregation that has always plagued the so-called unified Iraqi nation. This point may appear to be counterintuitive, as it may seem easier to conquer a country that is divided than a unified one, and indeed it is, but subsequent to victory in the battle, the war lies directly ahead. The war in this case is one in which Iraq is at odds with itself, and through the unraveling one finds a deeply divided nation—one that cannot be patched together by allied nations or the UN, as a sense of country can only come from the people themselves. Again, prior to the war, plans/schedules had to take into consideration that such possibilities were not only possible but rather inevitable when one looked to the past. The other perfect example is South Korea. US soldiers are still present along the demilitarized zone (DMZ) 50 years later! This kind of precedence must be considered and accepted, and it is not too late, even at this point in time, if proper actions are taken. It is up to the government to disseminate this information to the public through actions and innuendoes, and the media will slowly but surely drag it out into the mass public. The government will inevitably be ridiculed by the people and will later receive the cold shoulder, but if the president truly believes in the cause and the ripple effect a defeat would have on the future with respect to America's presence and view within the Middle East, he/she will have to risk his/her personal historical impact on the nation's well-being. One simply has to take a page from President Truman's book in order to understand. Soon after FDR died, Truman made the decision to fire nuclear weapons over Hiroshima and Nagasaki. He must have struggled madly with the idea, with the consequences, with his consciousness, and with his Christian teachings and upbringing. If he could in the end decide such a course of action, despite the consequences, all in the name of ensuring America's place in the world, then certainly this White House and the one to come can decide upon the withdrawal from or pursuit of victory in Iraq. The idea here is simple: this situation, though it may seem different from the past, still has much in common with it. It is up to the president and his cabinet to take key ideas from past conflicts and apply the modern touches required to achieve victory; but in the end, victory is still a possibility if one truly believes in the idea. The bigger question is, does the president still believe he can win, or is he waving the white flag?

Infrastructure can also serve as a two-way weapon against this formidable enemy. The allies could easily begin to build some of the absolutely necessary infrastructure, such as power plants or sewage plants, under the care and security required to ensure the safety of the workers. This would undoubtedly be an objective for the military to wrestle with, but once built, the plant would serve a means of providing the people with the essential services central to their families' existence and well-being. Those families will very quickly come to appreciate these vital necessities and would be very angry and disappointed with anyone that might interfere with any further progress or improvement. At this point, the allies will have won the appreciation of the people as well as their trust, which would force people to open up and provide essential information against the aggressor, the true aggressor, as they will have finally understood. This demonstrates how concrete action leads to concrete results.

The beauty of this option is that it can easily camouflage itself into a military playing card. If the enemy starts to fear the overwhelming positive reaction of the people toward the allies for their improvements to their daily lives, the enemy will then in essence be forced to destroy that piece of infrastructure provided by the allies. This would in turn outrage the people and inevitably turn them against their aggressor and into the arms of their true allies. This option again has two favorable outcomes, although it does have a downfall as well, and it too has two negative factors both highly dependent on the support of Congress and other allied governments. The first is financial, as the construction of a piece of infrastructure will be much more expensive than any structure built in the US. Contractors will have to be compensated for their work at four to five times the regular US salary, not to mention the logistics nightmare associated with the construction process. The other enormous problem is security, which plagues any project in the war zone. This kind of construction project will require a great deal of security forces or contractors that will have to be pooled from the already decreasing number due to Congress's current instruction. Regardless, if one chooses to pursue this option despite the difficulties, it could very well prove to be both a short- and long-term success.

There is one very key element that is often forgotten by the people regarding the war. It has somehow been thwarted by the mass media at large, over the country's dismay, especially given the degree of their access. The media in essence collectively succeeded in sensitizing the people toward the war, to the point where their direct involvement has literally paralyzed the people. The media's account of the death toll can be seen in two ways: one being an uplifting call to the people to rally for the cause for those who have fallen at the hand of the enemy, the other being the media's watchful eye on government action—though undoubtedly beneficial to their personal bottom line, it does unquestionably help produce a healthy equilibrium of checks and balances. Regardless of the notions mentioned above, the media is in many ways also responsible for the paralyzing effect that their coverage has had on the people. Their power is a double-edged sword! One must recall that the last two years to date have easily been a period of constant negative feedback on the progress of the war effort. It is so obvious that even the major broadcasts such as the NBC Nightly News have covered stories in which the anchor literally explains that the upcoming story will actually cover some of the "good" that is going on despite the violence at large. That constant negative energy is the same energy that will be fed to the military; a message of failure, uselessness, and the lost passage of time, if one is to come out of the war zone at all, in one piece. This passage, and the ideas not mentioned, is in no way a dagger in the back of the media, but simply a wake-up call to judge the manner in which this unquestionable form of communication can both aid and harm the aspirations for victory both at home and abroad. To that end, I still must seize this opportunity to thank those reporters in the field who are providing the incredible coverage of the war and have provided millions of great discussions at dinner tables around the world.

# CHAPTER 7

# Oil, the Black Ace

THE RESOURCE ONCE CONSIDERED the black plague transformed itself into the black ace virtually overnight, once its power was fully recognized and its necessity deemed absolute. It was as though salvation had come from the depths of the earth's core and fallen into the laps of the Arabic people, for the entire Arabic community to profit. Despite the underlying factor accompanying the riches, oil remains the cause behind atrocities playing out throughout the world, in the present and in the near and far-reaching future.

One undoubtedly sees a link between consistent oil supply requirements and conflict throughout the world. Whether the setting unfolds in Iraq, Saudi Arabia, or Venezuela, this resource has fueled such rage that its link to this scene and throughout history's scrapbook must be analyzed in the context of a means to the chosen end.

What one must understand and accept is that oil is not the problem. Again, one must exclude the context of global warming and other relevant environmental issues in order to accept what might appear to be a blind political/financial statement.

If one stands back and analyzes the situation from a third person's impartial point of view, under the cloudy gray skies of neutrality, one will quickly realize that the resource, if properly managed, is the ideal way to finance any viable idea with solid founding notions, toward its completion and success.

This will obviously not include every third-rate inventor's idea across the Arab world aimed solely toward personal success, though some will inevitably result with such riches, but rather those ideas that will directly and/or indirectly aid in the development of country and society.

One of oil's greatest powers lies in its ability to be used as collateral in acquiring loans to finance the immense number of projects that require funding throughout most of the Arab world

Oil becomes a tool of leverage in order to ensure almost any loan from any institution. Again as always, there is a catch. The constant flow of this precious resource must be ensured via constant vigilance from those in power. This will incur an extra cost, both financial and human, as many will perish to ensure production. Regardless, oil can be viewed not as the final answer upon which everything else is based, but rather as a transition that will take the people forward to a fully modern era of peace, stability, and economic freedom. Imagine oil as that ace that is held on to until finally, when revealed, it will allow for huge gains. It is then those winnings that must be put to good use in order to reach prosperity for all, otherwise condemning future people to the same hardships as those encountered in the past.

The importance of oil cannot be overstated, as it not only benefits the people of the Middle East, if properly administered by Arab leaders, but it fuels our lives and our bottom lines throughout the Western world. Without this resource, every transportation company, including all related companies providing services for these firms, would be virtually wiped out overnight. Think: every automotive, airline, and transport firm would cease to exist, creating an unemployment wave the size of which would be felt from New York to Tokyo. It would make the fiercest tornado pale in comparison to the shockwave and the terrible after-effects due to the seizure of oil production. There have been occasions of scarcity that have caused 10% to 20% increases in prices virtually in hours. What people must remember is that ensuring the stability of oil production not only helps the people in the Middle East, but helps us directly. So let us help one another, all the while ensuring the inception of new technologies that will relieve the pressure currently suffocating the industry. Furthermore, oil will provide much needed employment that pays for life's limitless wants and needs. In this case, the needs are of the greatest importance. Then once the people start to enjoy the wealth that comes with earning their livelihoods on a daily basis, they will come to detest any outside influence that would result in society's loss. In essence, oil and its wealth, when spread to the people at large, will help produce an internal struggle against the enemy to ensure the best interests of society. Oil will again become the ace if used properly by those in power.

Furthermore, one must recall that throughout history, the Arab people have never held such a prominent position at the table with their Western counterparts. Amongst all resources, oil has truly been the key to their establishment in Western society. This of course does not extend to the average Arab man and woman, but globally their presence is unquestionable.

As is the case, the fortune associated with this precious resource lies in its ability—if properly managed, of course—to lift the average man from poverty, in addition to its uncanny power to bring unquestionable wealth to the upper echelons of society. One must recall that in order to truly lift society from the depths of despair, several incremental steps must be completed, as opposed to a single jump from trough to peak. What must be conveyed to the mass public, via all media available, is that under the new government, funds will be properly budgeted to provide the training/instruction required to complete the numerous tasks associated with oil production/refinement and transport. This system, in its infant stages, must be monitored by an objective third-party organization that will properly manage funds and ensure reinvestment in the people. This might appear to be a cold, dry fact in the financial statements of oil firms, but it will translate into warm, soothing profitable reality for the people.

Again such incremental steps may appear to be overwhelming, but what is being suggested is synonymous with teaching a man to fish instead of simply feeding him for the day. Such small, significant actions could include the creation of classes for citizens who already have the education required, thus reducing the lead time associated with its implementation. Teach others smaller tasks or simply divide each task so that it becomes simpler and therefore easier to implement.

Obviously, the oil industry will have to do its part and will undoubtedly inherit risk associated with such a project, but they stand to inherit a fully functional production system monitored by the Iraqi people, a force much more powerful than US soldiers, as the people would be defending their very livelihoods, as opposed to US government oversight, whose very presence is at the mercy of Congress thousands of miles away from the production site/war zone.

It is up to Congress to therefore employ think tanks throughout the world, based both in engineering/logistical concepts as well as in financial profit-generating models, to propose a plan with a definite time span that would over its completed term provide success on all fronts, with all players then provided time to decide upon its acceptance or decline. Furthermore, the oil companies must be briefed throughout the process such that they remain aware of the progress made throughout, thus providing greater chances for final approval. The governments throughout the globe would then have to provide the security to ensure that the project will succeed, and given the highly favorable outcome for the region as a whole, there would be no reason for decline from any of the allies.

My suggestions are in many ways a rough model, but in the right hands they can help everyone involved, including the all-important investor, who can stand to profit immensely. In the end, the best plan is the one that favors the entire table.

Conversely, the world must remain in balance to ensure harmony throughout the system. Note that this collection of items is all-encompassing and includes political, scientific, sociological, and military affairs and their push against one another in their final quest for equilibrium. One must further note that final equilibrium is the key, not equality amongst the many participants, including the unknown that often trickles into the equation. As such, there are many downfalls to the oil industry that at times would appear to question the belief in balance altogether. The "black ace" is therefore in reference to oil as a whole because it is one of those obvious aces associated with Middle Eastern countries, all the while ushering in black clouds to those same people; of which there are many. Let us now analyze each of the negative aspects and turn them around so that they can be used to help as many of the participants as possible but with a constant reminder of the choice toward a specific outcome for both the region as well as the world at large. The two are obviously tied together very tightly.

The obvious problem remains one of greed and power, obtainable via the control of this particular industry. It just so happens that oil in many ways is the manner in which industry and manufacturing at large are "fueled," pardon the pun. The product itself has been dubbed "black gold," but I prefer the title I choose for this chapter, "the black ace," as it not only provides riches, it is the ultimate playing card by which all other stakeholders are directly or indirectly affected. The party that controls the flow, controls society; with such power comes many enemies, friends, and enemies that try to pass as friends. This fact is undeniable and cannot be changed unless the West builds friendships with oil-rich governments, or at the very minimum a relationship as friends in passing. As for those who would take the role as enemies, they in particular must be kept extremely close, in the best interests of national and international security and economic growth.

Despite the inability to reverse human nature's course, there are numerous significant layers involved that are far more damaging to oil's reputation, and they will continue to materialize throughout the Middle East. It is these very layers that cast a dark "black" shadow on an otherwise positive resource. If we start to "drill" through the layers, we immediately encounter the military struggle present directly resulting from the seizure and control of oil-rich terrains. The struggle is born as a result of the West's preoccupation with its required need for oil in an ever-demanding marketplace. One must recall that the demand in the past in no way mirrors today's fierce consumption rates. If one considers China alone and its oil requirements to sustain its immense growth taking place at this very moment, this standing alone, as the number two purchaser of oil exports, creates an overwhelming strain on the industry as a whole and on the US and other allies. The noose effect is forcing the Western allies into a nervous frenzy, with the US at the top of the list. These emotions are a principle factor and a central catalyst in the current Iraqi crisis. As this issue can never be subdued, if oil is to remain the foundation of our energy demands, the intensity of individual and collective governments will simply intensify until emotions spill throughout the Middle East.

This factor cannot change unless governments enact laws that will force the introduction of newer and cleaner energy alternatives. In many ways, this issue has reached a threshold, in which every possible and plausible factor is pointing away from oil production and toward renewable energies more local in nature. What local governments must do is tap into their state/provincial resources to alleviate some of the pressure associated with oil demand. For example, Quebec reduces its demand for oil, as it has a host of flowing rivers from which it can produce hydroelectric power and therefore provide energy to businesses and homes throughout the province and across borders to neighboring provinces and US states. The French have decided upon nuclear power to reduce their dependence on oil. In this case, it has opened a debate on the nuclear front, but they have managed to reduce their dependence nonetheless. Other alternatives include ethanol as a means to run cars and to power machinery. Geothermal sites can be set up throughout the world, as well as those for wind-propelled energy, as GE is currently promoting. There are many other solutions out there that collectively can reduce our dependence on oil, but despite which form best suits which locality, the idea is for each state/province, in each country, to place the onus on these possibilities so that they will indeed materialize. The idea in the end is that if we have other options available, we will not feel the noose around our necks, and this therefore reduces the probability of waging a battle or war based on energy requirements alone, as appears to be the case with the current situation in Iraq. Oil gives rise to yet another major struggle that affects the partisan's interaction between the different sects within Iraq. The three major groups are now fighting for the "Promised Land," if you will, which would inevitably grant enormous riches. The Shiites, Kurds, and Sunnis each believe that there is no time like the present to pounce on the opportunity. Prior to the fall of Saddam Hussein, the struggle was brutally controlled by the army, and therefore the blur between lines separating one group from the other was government controlled. In essence the war essentially created a shift with respect to control of the front lines between the different groups within the country. At the moment there is very little overlap between the different groups, with control having shifted from the government objective to a full-scale lethal intercommunity struggle. Perhaps the situation can be best described as the Wild West situated in a Middle Eastern setting. Regardless, of the current situation, this in no way pardons the atrocities committed by Saddam Hussein's government throughout his reign; it simply demonstrates the unbreakable law that states how energy can neither be created nor destroyed, only transferred from one form to another. What in fact will happen and in actuality is presently occurring is the creation of separate states within the country currently known as Iraq, and should the internal struggles continue, as enforced by this law and further solidified by human nature, the US and the entire world has literally ensured a constant oil crisis for its economic future. It is at this crucial juncture in time that allied forces must decide on the intended outcome and then stand by their decision with the proper means to ensure the chosen end, as opposed to having one dictated by exterior forces or, in this case, an interior one.

Once again, this situation is one in which the US and its allies can help themselves by helping the communities integrate, and if need be, integration should be encouraged, and if required, enforced. It might appear to be a brute strategy, but it is worth a try. With oil being the prime incentive, encouraging, better still voluntarily forcing, communities to integrate under the premiss that such actions would be in the best interests of their families. It will then force strangers, Kurds, Shiites, and Sunnis, into conversations and hopefully friendships over time. In the meanwhile, everybody will stand to profit from oil revenues, and who knows, maybe the black ace will demonstrate its tender, gentler side toward all the players at the table.

The bigger issue remains oil's direct effect on the politics of the Middle East for the next 50 years subsequent to the end of the current war. This dark ace will unquestionably then set the stage for a civil war that will deplete the very last resources of the people, including their will to fight. The situation will then reach the ideal point at which numerous neighboring states will decide to attack purely in the name of their own prosperity. This should not come as any surprise, as human nature knows no color, religion, or passport. In essence the national Iraqi map will undergo a transition period in which it will be first divided into the three countries followed by its assimilation into neighboring states such as Iran. This would provide Iran with immense control over a crucial resource for Western survival. This would in essence provide a lopsided negotiating power at the UN and possibility of terrorist sponsorship, though concrete evidence has not been provided by intelligence organizations worldwide as of yet.

The other possibility would be a scenario mirroring feudal times in which smaller areas were controlled by the lord and his men. Under this scenario, crucial oil wells would be protected at the expense of spilled blood at the surrounding boundaries. Imagine, if you will, a series of oil wells guarded by air and land against any attack that may be waged— soldiers literally stationed around lines in the sand simply to ensure the export of a liquid, the water of life tainted by the blood of men. This is yet another possible and plausible outcome for the Iraqi landscape and is in fact a microcosm of the current situation. All one has to do is simply imagine multiple "Green Zones" throughout the country defended for one purpose.

The realization of one of those possibilities, whether the former or the latter, or the union of the two, is one in which the local economies will cease to exist except for bartering at best, all resulting from the anarchy that would consume the already fragile structure currently in place. Furthermore, as with any society, as soon as the ability to conduct any form of commerce comes to a standstill, internal struggle, poverty, and disease will soon follow. One could picture abandoned cities, vast territories ruled by overlords. One must recall that oil was initially supposed to be accompanied hand in hand with wealth, but surely if proper means are not set forth into action, the chosen end will be dictated by the dark side of the playing card.

Perhaps one of the other effects of oil can be felt through the halls and open forums of the UN and NATO, where long-standing allies have become bitter, argumentative enemies as a direct result of the Iraqi war and therefore indirectly due to oil interests and their national assertions of its constant supply. This fact is perhaps even more dangerous, as it plays the role of divider and has essentially created two sides with respect to reasoning for war. One might stand back and express concern, as the central disagreement was purely over the context and grounds for a military incursion, but deep within the message, buried between layers and layers of political jargon, lies the black cloud, hovering like a fly on the wall of each and every debate. In order to win the war and therefore ensure the national interests of all those involved, the UN must come to an agreement that will ensure that key ingredient will be maintained at the status quo, i.e., the oil supply. As the situation currently stands, the US has no powerful allies to aid in the campaign. All of the allies that did provide support, such as England, Italy, and Spain, have felt the wrath of the people as these groups expressed and flexed their political rights to disagree with the current government's point of view. The reasoning is even deeper than the people realize, except that the beauty of human nature lies within. These people feel and sense the reasoning for war, with its foundation based purely on economic grounds, and though unable to express the idea in words, the emotion and outrage has surfaced within the significant majority of the eligible, voting public.

This point again can be overcome through open discussions among leaders, behind the scenes and away from high-visibility summits. Government must not forget how they can stand to profit and in turn pass on the stability to their peoples. The black ace, if properly managed, both militarily and financially, can profit all those seated at the table, but actions must be taken immediately to ensure that all those involved are properly and sufficiently compensated. In essence, the US must provide considerable incentives to ensure the aid of its allies, even if that means that they will realize a smaller slice of the pie. If not, this indecisive issue will haunt the US government and people for years to come and destroy any possibility of profit, whether political or financial, from the current crisis eroding the very core of America's political and economic presence throughout the globe. Perhaps one of the many lessons to be learned with respect to the oil industry as a whole lies in its link between the tangible and intangible qualities of this particular resource. If one studies the industry macroscopically, one quickly realizes oil's ability to link the economies of the world and thereby its respective peoples via its flow from point A to point B, and yet it is that very resource, or rather the control of that very resource, that serves that vital connection. It is as though this very flow of oil, from east to west, has somehow metamorphosed into a psychological wall separating one side from the other. In this context, no one side questions the importance of the "wall," as both communities use and abuse it in their best interests, yet that very wall is vital to both camps. What both sides fail to understand is that no such a barrier actually exists, except within the confines of people's opinions. The higher powers are thereby providing the psychological maintenance to ensure its stability and resistance against all those who would question its existence. After all, it is only within the last year or two that the green movement has truly gained momentum. It is these people that are threatening the very foundation of the "wall," just as the Berlin Wall was tested until it came crashing down. If this surge for an environmental renaissance continues, a need will be established, as opposed to absolute dependence, such that oil will again become profitable without being destructive and divisive. The green movement must therefore take place not only to clean the environment but more importantly to disarm an industry holding both parties hostage. Then once the need diminishes, the need to defend it will also slowly subside. Obviously in this scenario, oil companies stand to lose a great deal, but as Iraq becomes more and more dangerous and people continue to harbor psychological divisions further isolating East from West, companies can stand to gain for only so long before incurring immeasurable losses.

One must further dissect the known reserve quantities currently available in Middle Eastern countries in the context of their ability to provide for the generations that will come of age over the next 30 to 50 years. Recall that there has been much speculation as to the quantities available, especially if the constant rate of extraction is maintained or perhaps even increased, as the thirst for oil continues to grow at an alarming rate worldwide. Throughout this crucial period, oil will continue to be synonymous with great fortune, but as the years dwindle away, the dark side will once again appear and cast an immense shadow over the entire Middle East. Imagine, if you will, that period when there is so little oil remaining that no profit can be extracted, and the big companies finally decide to cut and run. The fortune tied to this resource will have finally been severed, and the principal load-carrying member ensuring relations between East and West will have failed under the economic and social stresses applied. More importantly is the devastation to the bottom line, as the population would be struck by a wave of unemployment that would far outweigh any hardships of the Great Depression of the 1930s felt all over North America. The powerful playing card will have transferred itself into the great misfortune for all generations within Iraq and the Middle East as a whole.

As the universe will then play its cards toward ensuring consistency, the Middle Eastern misfortune will then unquestionably be regulated by the profitable outcome throughout the rest of the Western world. The irony is that perhaps these possible turn of events are not at all random, but rather a means to a chosen end, as decided upon by Western governments to ensure power and stability for the future of their peoples. Is it not, and has it not always been, the number one objective for any government, kingdom, or empire throughout history? And so why would this major cornerstone of the present and future existence be any different? In essence this strategy is one in which the West will simply remove the founding power of the Middle East, by literally burning it away. The great aspect of this plan, if it is indeed the one set into action, lies in the willingness of Western governments to spread the wealth to the common man throughout the Middle East if and only if exterior forces are willing to allow the true peoples to simply work together so that everyone can profit from one of God's great gifts to this planet.

Regardless of the many ideas presented and explained throughout this chapter, the central idea stems from the time-tested truth that oil is both a blessing and a curse. It has come to be known as "black gold" by those who prosper from its use to the "black plaque" prior to the knowledge of its usage way back when. I prefer the title listed on the chapter heading, as it best describes its split personality. Furthermore, the inherent danger with this resource, as opposed to all others, remains its crucial link in the economic food chain. To lose this element would cause a wave stronger than any tsunami ever registered, as it would crush every industry from transport to materials to manufacturing.

As its stranglehold over society is so tight, governments must ensure the flow of economic life for all countries, but if one plays its cards right and minds its hand to ensure prosperity for decades to come, it will have provided the essential time required to produce the many alternatives necessary to power our insatiable need for energy. Accordingly, oil then becomes the wild card, a savior, to launch us into the next energy age if and only if we have the proper political minds making decisions that will better the standing of all. Only when we ensure the well-being of the majority does everyone stand to profit.

The second moral of this chapter and its influence on our chosen view of the future regarding our dependence on foreign oil production remains the absolute necessity for a transition period from the current oil-based economy to one built upon several energy alternatives. By producing a detailed schedule for this strategy, the current economy will thereby eliminate or drastically reduce our need for foreign oil and thus allow governments to make decisions based upon the best interests of their citizens and the international community, as opposed to the suffocating stranglehold that has been plaguing Western countries over the last half century. This point is of extreme importance, as the final decision for Iraq remains one based on this very fact. As for those who feel that government cannot follow through with such an ambitious plan, they only have to think of the time when President Kennedy proclaimed to all that a man, an American, would be on the moon by the end of the decade. Even the unimaginable, when broken down in small elements, can be achieved when it is the choice of those in power. All America has to do is decide and then follow through!

# CHAPTER 8

# *The Cost of War*

ONE OF THE DETERMINING factors in all wars despite any idea to the contrary remains the ability of the government to financially control costs while achieving the final objective, victory.

As this idea is never part of the inspiration for victory or valiant action on the battlefield, history has shown that poor financial performance with respect to control over spending and budget allocation has proven to be both fatal to the soldiers in the trenches and detrimental to the future of the national economy, as the burden will follow this and future generations to come. It is for this very reason that territories have fallen from one regime to another to the present status we see today.

One of the cold truths of war has always been an initial optimistic agenda toward victory that at the start appears to be a sustainable, financial endeavor for a fixed period of time, factoring in a given tolerance for error and the unknown. It is in the planning stages that the government, playing the role of the aggressor, chooses the final position of victory, partial victory, or failure, whether it be a conscious or subconscious act. One would argue that no government would ever knowingly enter a war doomed for failure, but in fact many have, as propaganda and emotion will often triumph over a financial prognosis completed by the treasury.

If you look back at this war or any past war, the initial budget automatically gives an indication as to the government's initiative and resolve for victory. Recall that Congress initially budgeted $80 billion for the war effort back in 2003. To any reader, it appeared to be quite a statement of its resolve for victory, and nothing less in Iraq but time then tested America's will by demanding yet another huge withdrawal (over another $80 billion) to continue to finance the goal. All of a sudden, as in every war, doubt creeps into the plans and often alters the definition of victory to ensure the mission viability as well as a reasoning and compensation for the losses incurred. The president and the entire government, whether Democrat or Republican, then found themselves in the fourth year of the campaign having spent almost a half a trillion dollars and were no doubt reassessing their future plans. Now, subsequent to all the emotion and outcries for or against the initial approval for war, the head of the treasury shares center stage with other relevant military leaders to explain what the government can and cannot afford in its plans for a chosen end for the country.

It is at this point that the enemy begins to smell blood and transitions from its past role as prey to the current and future role as predator, all resulting from financial miscalculations that are leading and will continue to lead toward the realization and final submission to failure's chokehold. In essence it is emotion and belief in the cause that result in victory, but most often it is superior financial planning that truly sets the stage for success.

As the situation stands, the current government has failed in the planning stage as it suggested that the need for this campaign was dire and that Iraq needed to be disarmed immediately. In hindsight, the cost of the war had to have been projected in one form or another, with a budget to include the possibility of failure. After analyzing the effect of the "worst" scenario, excluding the possibility for nuclear war and its cost on government, it was precisely then that it should have acted with financial responsibility in mind, by ensuring the approval of the UN Security Council in order to divide the costs amongst its allies and thereby ensure victory both financially and politically, if for no other reason than the dry financial facts provided in the event of a unilateral campaign.

Another major factor to be considered in this or any situation in which a military solution is to be set forth is the voluntary or involuntary submission to tunnel vision. The government cannot make a case for war without considering the infinite problems that may result from the task undertaken. This government chose to concentrate on the incursion alone without analyzing the effects from the macroscopic and microscopic points of view. Note, this does not imply that the Republican party did not provide a litmus test to understand the implication of failure and the ripple effect throughout the world; their actions simply appear to be those associated with a "tunnel vision" mindset. Imagine, if you will, a train traveling through the great wilderness, prior to the conductor's decision to either continue on the track under the open skies or to pass through the manmade tunnel carved out of an approaching mountain range. This party, along with the support of the opposing Democrats, choose to go through the tunnel and ignore all the information as stimuli available under the open skies. This was exactly the decision the government had to avoid as, if one continues with the analogy, the government would have received all the signals pointing toward their true objective—Afghanistan.

On the other hand, one must be objective and applaud the resolve of the president and Republican party, at least at the start of the mission. In war, once it has been declared, it is that very tunnel vision that is required for victory, and that form of thinking has been a key point clearly associated with the Republican party, as opposed to their opponents on the other side of the aisle. Of course, this was not always the case with Democratic representatives, as the Kennedy and FDR administrations clearly demonstrated.

On another front, when one chooses war and victory (at least in the initial stages), there is an unquestionable human cost associated with dead and wounded soldiers who will carry out the orders. A president must be impartial and do what is in the best interests of the country, but he/she must never forget or take advantage of the loyalty of the fighting forces. The question had to have been asked at some point in time as to the projection of casualties that would accompany the mission. Was the information providing the grounds for war accurate, believable, and consistent with what other intelligence organizations were expressing at the time as well? We have seen certain cases in which the government made it clear that victory, or at least secrecy, outweighed any cost. Take, for example, a certain undercover CIA/political couple, whose identity was leaked to the papers, when disagreements with final assessments for the war resulted in a breach of national security for all intents and purposes when the wife's CIA identity was leaked to the papers. Was the mission so important that victory was to be achieved at all costs, and thus those at fault in the government felt that the ends justified the means?

In addition to the above-mentioned facts, one cannot help but realize that at the very start of the incursion, the entire arsenal was made use of during the so-called "shock and awe" campaign. While this strategy has definite merits, it has great faults as well, as there is an immediate spike in cost as total chaos breaks out. If one is fortunate enough, the assault will crush the defending forces such that their will to fight extinguishes as the initial surge dies down. But, as one would imagine, there was no such luck, as the forces regrouped into small militias around Baghdad and the rest of the country. At this point, the government could only hope that the enemy had decided to flee to neighboring countries, allowing US forces to settle and begin the rebuilding of the new nation. Perhaps in a perfect world, such a scenario would be possible, but in reality, even in the best of cases, a transient period would follow. Regardless, from a financial point of view, a realistic, updated algorithm could have been implemented to estimate the cost associated with the incursion. It is here that one should have referred to the last military disaster taken, namely Vietnam. That war alone could have been used as a perfect model upon which to base a modern military failure. The government could have requested the opinions of mathematicians and financial consultants to map the worst-case scenario for this war from its start to an end, ranging from 1 to as many as 10 years. The algorithm could have included such variables as troop increases, sudden foreign troop additions, and abrupt US troop and hardware losses due to ambushes, all based on past experience.

Despite those who might second-guess such statistical calculations, one would at the very least understand the implication of time, true populations, foreign aid, and scheduled loses, whether they occur in reality at the same rate or not. The idea here remains the ability to ensure that the economy can indeed sustain scheduled losses over a given period of time but even more importantly provide some form of timeline as to the point where the effort simply becomes too expensive to pay for.

Obviously, a government cannot base its decision for war purely on a financial level, as its reasoning is extremely complex and cannot be based on a single factor. Conversely, if the reasoning for a particular cause for war is not founded, its projected costs will inevitably uncover all the holes associated with its makeup. So, if one was to return to the days just prior to the very start of the war and present a realistic budget of a losing war based on the definition by military analysts and mathematicians, one would quickly realize how the decision to go ahead would inevitably paralyze any additional action against any other targets for the next 5 to 10 years. This is in direct reference again to Afghanistan, as it remains the true target that was set aside because the government felt Iraq was the central target. In the meantime, the paralysis of US forces allowed other enemies of the state to strut their power, knowing America's inability to consolidate any forces for incursions elsewhere. In financial terms, the government acted like a young, inexperienced investor who mismanaged her portfolio by allocating too great a share to a single investment without taking into consideration others that might come along, not to mention the loss in net value if that significant investment should falter.

Furthermore, if we continue to analyze the situation from a financial standpoint in order to aid allied forces toward victory, one quickly realizes that in addition to simply increasing the funds to finance the missions, one can wage a financial war by seizing any and all suspicious transfers to persons who may be deemed a threat to national security. If such a policy were to be instated, as is most probably the case, one would have to rigorously monitor the severity of the program to ensure its integrity and intent toward the chosen end.

Under this scenario, different task forces would be set up around the globe under the supervision of the International Monetary Fund (IMF), with the strict purpose being the interception of funds to terrorist organizations worldwide. Most importantly, with the help of law enforcement and gifted programmers, specific codes could be enabled, tagging suspicious transactions that would then be investigated by trained financial personnel. Then under those circumstances, where there is believed to be a transfer to terrorist organizations, the information would be passed on to Interpol and national agencies to apprehend the possible terrorists.

This same idea could be implanted to ensure that funds raised for any charities throughout particular regions be monitored to ensure that the destination for the funds is as promised. One might consider charities in which huge amounts of cash are raised, portions of which are in liquid currencies that can then be pooled together to purchase arms and equipment on the black market.

Perhaps the point of greatest interest resides with local government's ability to track the threat from within. Using such a system, even at its inception, could very quickly provide governments with estimate locations of cells throughout the country, thus providing a refined investigation tool for law enforcement. Furthermore, when data begins to accumulate with respect to supplying funds, governments can analyze the data with the goal of equating peaks and troughs with time of danger and tranquility. Perhaps such data could also give ideas as to the lead time and funds required to finance a mission, battle, or war once all the data are compiled and analyzed macroscopically and microscopically. Obviously this form of prevention will most certainly not cause any opponent to fall, but its interference in the enemy's financing is undoubtedly an interesting and worthwhile exercise to undertake.

In addition to the above-mentioned costs associated with any military incursion, one must both realize and accept that when exiting a war, either voluntarily or involuntarily, there are plenty of costs that further aggravate and erode the already delicate financial and emotional state of the military, the people, and the economy. Recall that there is always a cost with the displacement of military forces that begins well in advance of the first or hardware displacements. As the current strategy in place appears to be one of defeat, the apparent chosen end to the war has military analysts feverishly working on a well-devised escape plan. Regardless of its success, there is a cost associated with the decision that will mount in the millions and probably hundreds of millions throughout the effort of slowly removing troops.

If one analyzes the withdrawal costs, the bill would include thousands of hours for the military personnel planning the exit, followed by the creation of a schedule that would be submitted to each of the branches of the armed forces. Those orders would then trickle down to all personnel that will complete the manual labor. As this procedure will be criticized by every major government worldwide, the rate of troop withdrawals will be anything but quick, as the US government will aim to minimize its failure to complete the initial objectives. This very idea will lead to substantial financial losses, which in comparison with the $500 billion spent will appear to be minimal but are by no means excusable, especially as they are interpreted as direct losses without profit, taken directly from the same pot that could otherwise provide for the many programs that could make use of those very funds.

As the financial importance of the withdrawal will have reached an apex, the exodus of personnel from the war zone will again create another major problem with respect to the security of US forces that continue to occupy posts as their comrades begin to be shipped out. This leaves US forces at the mercy of the militias who would be studying their movements in order to crush any last hope of salvaging a lost cause. Recall that this is the chosen end, and these are the means by which the government will bring that idea into existence. The only difference here is that the death of soldiers between the time the withdrawal begins to the moment the last soldier retrieves the flag from the nearby flag posts will have been in vain, with the number of deaths directly related to the planning and therefore inherently with the financial planning and funds allocated to this endeavor by the government. In essence, one must spend taxpayer money to continue to finance a losing war, in which an astronomical amount of money has already been spent with yet another increase to ensure the safe withdrawal of troops during the exit as decided upon by the government and the people.

The irony of this fact is that in the case of the losing incursion, one in which victory or partial victory is not attainable, at least according to current estimates and current mindsets, I believe that those funds transferred would be some of the first that would be welcomed by the American public. This turns out to be one of those cases where financial motivation must be overlooked to ensure the well-being of the men and women who have valiantly fought on behalf of the government's wishes in the aid and protection of American interests and for the unwavering respect for the country; this variable and the accompanying losses must be willingly overlooked.

The general public must also come to terms with the cost associated with financing the medical needs of wounded soldiers, which includes not only those with physical ailments but those with mental and emotional problems as well. This is one of those costs that is very expensive, and by no means should the budget ever be considered to be a burden to the government and the people. It is the duty of the people to help the soldiers who have paid a tremendous physical, psychological, and emotional price in the defense of their country, regardless whether the campaign was just or not. This same idea must be extended to the families of those who lost a loved one overseas, as more than 3,000 families can attest to. These people will never again see that person except for the afterlife, and as such, they must be compensated for their loss. Just imagine all those families which in most cases lost the principal breadwinner and now must cope with not only the emotional struggle but also the financial one. The government's response of a few thousand dollars for each of these families' losses will in no way provide any consolation for them. Since the government is an entity, and not an actual person, it is via the presidents' handling of monetary compensation for families of fallen soldiers that it could truly show its respect and gratefulness for their sacrifice. Note, this act alone would cost the government and thus the people over $3 billion if one was to give $100,000 tax free to each of the families that lost a loved one in battle. This is an ever-growing nonrecurring cost, as the KIA (Killed In Action) figure was over 3,000 in 2006, to say nothing of the many bloody months that have ensued since. To further add to the growing cost for war, coverage was just recently aired on news stations regarding the dreadful conditions of veterans care housing, in which everything from the floors to ventilation needed to be fixed in order to provide proper care for patients trying to recover from their wounds. This is one of those intolerable situations that once again calls for immediate funding as the number of veterans continues to grow by the thousands and will continue to require medical attention.

One must recall that as it is the government's decision to wage war, it is that very choice that resulted and affected the futures of thousands of soldiers. As such, the government is not only forced to act out of duty for its wounded, but must do so as an expression of gratitude and thus voluntarily choose to provide a comfortable end to a soldier's haunting ordeal.

Another significant cost directly associated with the war effort remains the daily cost of the numerous products, vehicles, communication devices, etc., used throughout the battlefield. As there had been no major incursion for years prior to the current crisis in Iraq, there was no doubt as to the substantial inventory of military hardware that could easily be used for any and all types of military situations. Regardless, as the inventory begins to decline, thus reducing levels to an optimum status, one could quickly realize that past a certain critical point, the overall inventory must be ensured at a direct cost to the government and therefore the taxpayer.

One can easily surmise that at the start of the war, a very small percentage of the inventory was being sent very quickly without any question, but as the war drags on, its ability to meet the needs of both the war effort and its previous engagements already promised quickly begin to reduce the overall value of this precious account. Most importantly, the losses incurred in the almost daily battles include helicopters shot down while providing aid to soldiers in the field, or tanks ambushed during a fatal drive on the return to the war zone, as well as the extraordinary amounts of ammunition used every hour to complete the tasks. These are nonrecurring losses that can never be recovered, an absolute financial loss in every sense of the word.

This form of thinking may appear both cold and completely disconnected from the emotional aspects of war, but it is exactly this form of thinking and estimating that could have provided a case against the need for war from a financial standpoint when the incursion was first proposed. Again, one must understand that the cost associated with the depletion of the military inventory is by no means a case for war, but if you go through and add up the numerous costs included in this chapter alone, not to mention the hundreds of other small-ticket items, one can quickly mount a powerful financial case against the need for war. In addition, in cases where military force is indeed necessary and truly founded in principle, this preoccupation would simply disappear into the background. In those cases, such as World War II, the means justified the chosen end, and so any financial reasoning simply did not apply. Regardless, this crisis appears to be one of those particular errors in judgment whose very foundation could quite possibly have been shaken by a sound cost analysis.

As such, qualitative analysis has been inferred with respect to a negative financial return from the very start of the American incursion in Iraq. There is also an unquestionable and extremely profitable motive for war as well—one that is deeply rooted in the necessity to fund an insatiable defense contracting industry that must reinvent itself from cycle to cycle. With respect to this industry, crests lie between a full cycle marking the time span between the start and end of battles and full-blown wars. It is within the overlapping research and production cycle that defense firms both create as well as sell the technology that will be used by military forces in the war zone. It is these firms that owe their very existence to military conflicts and therefore in many ways require consistent and periodic arguments requiring either the application or the display of force to showcase the new technology they have created. If one analyzes even deeper, it is war or the preparation for possible war that creates the demand for wartime products and technology. This demand then forces defense companies to provide new technology, all the while requesting increased production rates, thus forcing firms to hire new personnel for research and development as well as production, directly impacting the financial well-being of society for hundreds of thousands of workers throughout the Western world. Obviously, those people then pump dollars into other sectors of the economy, closing the economic loop.

Not only does the war and its effort help the working person occupying the many positions in industry, not to mention the soldiers in the field, but the attention to the industry will also provide a great deal of profit with respect to stock value for those involved in the stock market and its volatility. As with any big industry, there are always those who will push for a certain turn of events and will directly or indirectly benefit from the financial standing of their personal portfolios. These individuals will profit immensely from the increased dividends per share or the rising stock value due to the staggering number of stock options included with their inflated paychecks. It is this select group of individuals that must be monitored very closely, as their actions could be added fuel to the fire and thereby create the case for war and thus their profit as a result.

This in no way lays blame on the heads of the defense contracting industry, as it is America's enemies that are shifting the spotlight on themselves by disobeying the international arms treaties set forth by the United Nations. These so-called rogue states are their own worst enemies, but it is up to those in power to ensure, to the best of their abilities, that the discussions for war revolve around the issue of national security and not the exponentially increasing figures of personal bank accounts. In other words, the government and the people must cast a watchful eye over the defense industry to ensure the outcome envisioned, as opposed to a one-sided industry-based outcome.

To summarize the actions, this government, and any government throughout history for that matter, has always revolved around the health of its treasury prior to making any decisions with respect to any and all military incursions that would tie down its forces for a lengthy period to come as well as require substantial funding to finance the effort undertaken. Furthermore, history will at times force a country to defend itself, while on other occasions it will require a final decision to attack at the so-called optimal point; regardless, there is an unquestionable and an unavoidable cost that will accompany the chosen route, and the financing of the journey, whether it ends in victory or defeat, should be clearly stated and justified in order to begin and complete the journey toward the chosen end.

# CHAPTER 9

# Choosing to Mend the Ties

THE ACTIONS, DISCUSSIONS, DISAGREEMENTS, quarrels, innuendos, and carefully crafted suggestions were all in an effort to somehow align foreign opinion with US plans prior to the Iraqi invasion. The numerous heated arguments among the founding members of the United Nations reached explosive levels, to a point where great friendships that had been forged over time and past hardships were tested and sometimes severed altogether, simply because of Republican ill-founded beliefs that war in Iraq was an absolute necessity toward the ultimate goal of national security of the country and UN member states.

In order to now understand what actions must be taken in order to mend the ties, one must first see and understand the pitfalls that occurred prior to, throughout, and during the current conflict.

One must recall that subsequent to 9/11, the US government had unprecedented access from numerous governments around the world as never before in its history. It was as though the Bush White House had carte blanche with respect to its ability to acquire foreign military aid in its quest for the arrest of Osama Bin Laden and the associated terrorist groups that he represented. This aid was not only of a military nature, but also included intelligence from foreign agencies and most importantly the coalescence of the international community around the US president. Never before had the peoples around the world been so sympathetic to the US situation.

Then after receiving aid from the international community for its plans in Afghanistan, as well as aid from Pakistani president Mousharof for aid along the Pakistani border, the government decided to set the country's political, economic, and military future on a tangent to the then well-laid plans that had been set in motion. It was at that point that the government began to present a link between the War on Terror and the Iraqi situation; one that was supposedly of grave nuclear proportion. It was then that foreign governments as well as the UN asked for calm, as the Iraqi situation had been under the microscope since the previous Bush presidency and did not appear to be linked directly with the 9/11 terrorist plot or the supposed nuclear threat due to the trafficking of nuclear materials from Niger. This was of course followed by then Secretary of State Colin Powell's presentation at the UN for the US case for war. The flat-out rejection gave rise not only to the principally unilateral effort that is presently taking place in Iraq, but also the official point in time at which the disagreements throughout the world backfired and dissolved any and all public opinion in favor of the US. Since then, US relations have hit new lows in line with its economic state.

Now the true test subsequent to the abbreviated course of past events must be set forward to mend the relationships between allied countries within the UN and request their help depending on the strategy chosen. Regardless, if we backtrack to the start of the military incursion, there are several points in time at which the US government could have received foreign aid and capitalized on its initial positive position. Recall the "march" to Baghdad, in which US forces literally made their way in Hummers, jeeps, tanks, and on foot. After arriving, liberating the people from their tyrannical leader, President Bush could have requested while riding the high tide that foreign aid would be welcomed for the remainder of the mission. It was at this point that greed entered into the calculation, as the government saw this as an opportunity to show the world America's might on the battlefield, and even more so, America's ability to complete the mission on its own without the help of its seemingly bureaucratic allies at the UN. What they failed to realize was that the chosen end was not victory in battle, but victory over the war for the welfare of the people and the stabilization of the country, and of course the return to stability of the oil industry. One must note that this was an ideal point in time, as the US shortly after managed to receive military aid from both Italy and Spain. It was at this very point that the US had to play the role of the responsible elder statesman who shares the riches with its allies despite past arguments.

It is very possible that given the then positive advances that had taken place, the French, Russians, and Germans might have changed their minds, as shifts in thinking occur all too often on the political stage.

The US could have also capitalized one other time on that infamous fateful weekend when the proper intelligence led it to a hole in the ground that contained a then precious and invaluable commodity: President Sadam Hussein. This was the US's last opportunity to use its findings for international support, and yet again the government did not use the fruits of its labor to acquire aid for its fighting forces.

Obviously from that point on, the military effort has almost continuously resulted in minimal or marginal returns at best, with the exit of the few allied troops (Italian/Spanish) that were present, under the political heat associated with the growing discontent over troop losses in the region. In fact, President Bush's decision for war then resulted in political losses for Prime Minister Blair in England, Prime Minister Berlusconi in Italy, and Prime Minister Anzar in Spain. The last hope of acquiring aid presented itself in November of 2004, as the presidential elections came to a close. In this case, it was the American people that shot themselves in the foot by deciding to choose President Bush for a second term when Senator Kerry was undoubtedly the ideal candidate for the job. There was even talk of a French entry onto the battlefield if a "proper" leader were in charge! Then much to the dismay of many of the peoples around the globe, the American public decided with a reasonable margin that President Bush deserved a second term. In many ways these last three years of bloodshed are as much an acceptance from the people as was the president's decision to continue the effort.

Again, hindsight is 20/20, but the idea of governments aiding the Bush call for war was clearly political roulette. Despite these past facts, let us now look ahead and examine how those ties can once again be mended.

At this point, there is no use arguing over spilled milk, as the continental divide is firmly in place. Perhaps a better description for the current status of US diplomacy would be more in line with the Hawaiian islands: lonely and isolated from surrounding opinions, despite all it has to offer. The central question therefore remains, what actions must be taken by US diplomats all the way up the chain of command to president in order to bring back the shine and luster on US diplomacy?

One must recall that in addition to isolating itself from the vast majority of its neighbors, the US government also created a continental divide in Europe, in which the five major countries collided in their beliefs with respect to providing aid to America. The disagreement literally tore the European landscape into two camps, for and against, with England, Italy, and Spain providing aid, while France and Germany forcefully abstained. It was this same disagreement that literally caused the eventual political downfall of all three leaders previously alluded to. In addition to the divide overseas, this disagreement included another nontangible division along the 45th parallel, when Canada and then Prime Minister Chrétien opposed US action and despite all criticism remained true to his word and to the country that aid would not be provided by the Canadian armed forces unless concrete evidence was brought to light. Note that from a US standpoint, having Canadian support would not only have provided legitimacy to the mission, as Canada has consistently chosen and acted in line with the best interests of all involved, but the Canadian prime minister would have provided the bridge between Europe and the US that was crucial to any possible agreement that could have been reached. These notes are worth mentioning, as they too could have changed the current situation in Iraq; but again I digress, and must return to possible solutions as opposed to dwelling on the past, as only then can plans be drawn in the hopes of salvaging a sinking freighter.

It is at this point that my criticisms turn the corner from pessimistic to constructive, in hopes that even a few of the suggestions set forth may be put into action, as the current US diplomatic situation is in dire need of forceful, action-minded solutions to overcome the overwhelming inertia tying it down.

As there is a great deal of pressure against any major decision on the Iraqi front currently on the table, it would be in the best interest of US diplomatic status, and therefore the American people, that diplomats attack the smaller and simpler problems currently requiring foreign aid. This is a simple suggestion, but it is exactly what is needed to start a fluid dialogue, to once again travel back and forth between the US and those allies that resented recent actions committed by this government.

Moreover, it will once again put the US and its allies on the same side of the table and will indirectly cause a bonding/healing process that usually occurs between friends. Furthermore, if US diplomats can join a consecutive number of these "simpler solutions," a momentum will begin to develop in US favor that is completely eluding them at this time. Again, this suggestion is based purely on the idea that the US currently finds itself at the bottom of a hole and is unable to claw its way out.

Furthermore, it is now in America's best interest to cherry-pick a topic of international relevance and back those same allies that so fervently opposed the US position in Iraq, mainly France, Germany, and Russia. Once again, it would be on a topic of low to medium importance but one that will clearly pass the message between governments that this president and this government understand and are willing to work together to make the best of a bad situation. This same position would be followed with a maximum collaboration on as many future projects as possible that are currently under consideration.

Perhaps one of the greatest forms of forgiveness on the political stage, to truly show that the morale is indeed soaked into the psyche of the government, would lie in US aid for existing UN plans that it initially declined in the past. It would be an exercise for US diplomats to research and once again cherry-pick an issue, perhaps a ruling of the international court, that it declined and provide reasoning that would allow for providing aid to one of its feuding allies. This would be a show of solidarity between allies, while the US retains its initial position, all the while allowing spectators to observe the reconciliation process.

Then once trust has entered into the equation once again, the US could then demonstrate that it has learned from its mistake on the Iraqi diplomatic front by providing to its respective colleagues the additional evidence that it may have had and did not present during then Secretary of State Colin Powell's address to the UN. This evidence may not be a sound judgment but it would stop any further questioning that remains with respect to the possible evidence that existed. In the case that no further evidence exists apart from that shown, that would be a sign that the government was forthcoming with information and truly wants to turn the page on the current view of US diplomacy. Either way, it will improve the dismal condition of foreign opinion of recent US political decisions. Here too it is a case where information of this importance would be reserved only for those of the highest office, such that proper action for a possible shift in national opinion would come from the apex down.

Only subsequent to the actions mentioned above, whether all suggestions are followed or only in part, can fruitful decisions take place on the explosive issues of Iraq, including troop scheduling, exit strategy, current US and foreign troop levels, and future action with respect to Iran's movements and reactions to the crisis.

In addition, the US could begin to receive aid by simply asking for opinions for the "proper" course of action from nations with veto power that initially resisted the call to arms in 2003. This simple action would transfer the limelight as well as the pressure to its allies, thus converting the US position from outsider to team player in an instant. More importantly, it would force French, German, Russian, and Chinese diplomats to come up with alternatives that could be set forth whether they are in accordance with US option or not. This will also allow the US to share the pressure with its allies, without causing a drastic shift in short-term plans. It would be during this time that the White House could propose the need to stay the course, as plans would be brewing amongst the team of minds throughout the UN. In essence, the time required to create, summarize, and mold the final statements from the individual or collective governments would buy some time as well as provide the small window of opportunity to put into action any last effort at fortifying the situation on the ground in Iraq.

Furthermore, subsequent to UN findings, one of the countries may set forth scenarios in which a possible extension of the timeline is recommended for US oversight alongside other UN troops with the idea of a smaller, more focused goal in mind. The ideas that the other countries would pose could be anywhere from a speedy six-month complete withdrawal to the fortification of small districts organized around specific, lucrative drilling sites and transportation routes. The main idea here is for other nations to feel the pressure of the dilemma faced by the US government, despite the fact that the situation is purely of its own making. Furthermore, if the exercise results in few ideas from UN participation, the US could in fact use that lack of creativity as a reason to continue with the mission as is. These are again only suggestions, but the government will weigh every option or outcome, and leverage to its advantage.

Despite all diplomatic action taken, there is no objection to the government use of backdoor channels through which certain agenda items can be accomplished, cases for war solidified, and nuances silenced. It would be through these backchannels that intelligence agencies worldwide would collaborate to uncover weak military positions and possible nuclear threats to the homeland, the definition of which would now include the landmasses of all the allies, just as President Kennedy proclaimed during the Cuban Missile Crisis that an attack by the Soviet Union on any of its allies would be considered an attack on the United States. Note that this idea of sharing information, though already in existence, must be monitored to ensure its continued success, especially given the times. At this point, US goodwill must be met with UN action acknowledging both publicly and behind the scenes that wounds are beginning to heal. In order to do so, the UN would schedule periodic and calculated actions in the region and throughout the world, sending the irrefutable signal that the coalition is once again aligning toward a common goal. One of the greatest contributions the UN could provide to the US for the many times in which it came to the aid of others throughout its history could be expressed via an elaborate exit strategy in which allied nations would provide aid to US forces on the ground to minimize casualties throughout the exit period. This could come via an exit strategy that maximizes the efficiency of current US forces throughout their exit based on their location, number, distance from a friendly border, etc. This strategy could also include small numbers of foreign troops that would take up preparatory roles that simply eat up crucial US manpower. These same troops can be embedded with US units to ensure escape routes set up by US forces and perhaps provide additional escape routes previously unknown to the US military.

These countries could also explain to the heads of state believed to be aiding terrorist groups that should their soldiers be hurt during the exit, political ties with those allies would suffer setbacks, not to mention the military response from the UN as a whole should their soldiers encounter mass casualties during the exercise.

The key note to emphasize on the political front to any and all spectators, including terrorist groups and any sympathizers walking along the fine line, undecided as to their participation, remains the essential raison d'etre for the UN: to maintain order throughout the world within a reasonable, allowable, and tolerable range. Therefore, despite arguments between key members of the union, once one member takes it upon itself to display its willingness to accept the consequences of past decisions and takes the necessary steps to mend the ties with its allies, the duty of all states is to support the best strategy set forth for the best interests of all members. That sense of union will set a precedent for any terrorist organization with the intent of disturbing the plans set forward.

In addition, the UN could quite simply provide financially, by making use of a percentage of its budget to either aid the US or help pay for the effort of its forces. This of course would be the equivalent of throwing money into a deep, dark hole, but it would nonetheless be a show of support. Furthermore, the UN could provide translators to the Pentagon to decipher and translate messages seized by intelligence agencies and to accompany US soldiers in areas where the military must communicate with the public. This has been a weak spot for the US government throughout the entire affair and will very quickly pay dividends.

The UN could also extend its bureaucratic might by communicating with OPEC and asking for its cooperation and influence throughout the world in order to have increased production where there is less volatility so that the current demands can be sustained. This again would provide a short-term fix and would buy some time while the US exits the region, thus avoiding two explosive problems from occurring at the same time, as this strategy appears to be the favorable approach on Capitol Hill.

The organization could use its influence through member-nation representatives and request logistical aid for upcoming offensives that would provide cover for existing forces. Such would include military bases in strategic locations such as those off the Sicilian coast or even more so from airbases along the Turkish/Lebanese/Jordanian border. The use of these locations would justify the chosen end, as the exit strategy will be advertised throughout the Arab world as the fleeing of infidels from their land, and therefore any aid from certain allies would be overlooked because of the success associated with the big picture. In the end, despite all the strategy associated with the exit of US forces from the region, it is plain and simple to see, understand, and feel the huge US loss on all fronts from this particular military exercise, but I will leave this discussion for the final chapter.

A similar suggestion would be set forth to all members in the region with respect to their influences on the strategic situation across each of the respective borders. This is one of those cases where measurable consequences must be explained and invoked upon any country's direct or indirect aid or facilitation of entry of terrorist groups into Iraq. Such action would limit outside influence as well as allow the UN to locate troops at specific locations along the numerous borders of which both Syria and Iran could pose the greatest threat. As these borders are immense and cross desert landscapes, member nations could help by providing technologies to help monitor the areas of high risk. These could include additional satellite imagery from Russia, for example, or new advanced technologies for monitoring sections of border crossing. Note that those new technologies would not only help the cause by minimizing illegal intrusions, but would provide the optimal setting for any companies to showcase an existent technology that could be purchased by government and companies around the world. The implications are endless and stand to be extremely profitable for any company able to provide such a system. As can be seen, these suggestions are merely an exercise in mending the broken ties between the US and the allies, as opposed to the actual decision for Iraq's future, which has yet to be decided upon. Regardless, with the US gearing up for an exit strategy, at least for the time being, these suggestions, or something similar, will have to be decided or acted upon via a back and forth exercise so that future crises can be dealt with as a solid unified organization, as opposed to two divided entities. In other words, the exercise of compromise over the failed Iraqi endeavor will prepare the allies for a standoff with Iran should tensions elevate to a boiling point. In other words, if one looks at the big picture, the US and the allies would be choosing to forget US actions in the best interests of national security, for all member nations, if a military incursion into Iran would be required, should the nuclear threat reach intolerable levels. In this case, the commitment and collaboration required to undertake the grand objective would be both extraordinary and one of the most delicate and sensitive missions since World War II. Given the implication of a possible future Iranian crisis in keeping with the context of both the chapter and the theme of this "capolavoro," why not voluntarily choose to mend the ties not just with European allies, Russia and China, but with Iran as well? Extend the olive branch of goodwill to the enemy through small calculated steps in the beginning, leading to a great crescendo: the suspension of the US embargo on products from and to Iran. This might appear to be a great shift in US doctrine on relations with this particular country and would raise further questions as to its relations with other countries such as Cuba that would have to accompany this decision in parallel. Regardless, the US must realize that sometimes, to remain in power, one must loosen the grip in order to decrease the pressure, before it reaches explosive levels.

Choosing to mend the ties with countries like Iran would create a new market for US companies. It would create an efficient flow of oil to the West and most importantly would demonstrate to the Iranian people the goodwill of an ally, as opposed to the iron fist of the imperialist power, as is the projection of Washington from the people in Tehran and all over the country. Of course, each step the US takes to mend the ties must be met with a response from Tehran as well, in order to create the balance required for the peace to come. All the while, the military option is never removed from the US playbook; it is simply one of the cards at the bottom of the heap, silent and draped over by the others that will add to the well-being and stability of the entire region and the entire world. In essence, this manner of thinking would turn the tide on the Iranians by showing everyone that the US is doing everything in its power to direct the future toward a peaceful setting—that it would be up to the Iranians to act in the best interests of their people and shift them toward a successful future firmly based in economic and political stability. In keeping with a topic comprehensible to all, one can easily understand and agree with experts who estimate that the cost of a barrel of crude to climb to the heights of $200 should a war erupt in Iran over the many currently unresolved issues. Not to mention the added pressure this would cause on other sites throughout the world, as others such as President Chavez, for example, try to capitalize on the weak US state that would result from its actions with respect to Iran. This would further create an economic depression of the greatest magnitude, as oil remains the pillar upon which the US economy is based.

Basically, the US must ensure that it always remains the body that controls the discussion by acting and directing the situation as required in order to continue to have the upper hand, at least for the near future anyway. Regardless, should this government and the future government take on the role of a reactionary state, all of the work completed to date will have been lost. In reality, actions of the defensive nature would not only distance both countries and the UN from a peaceful future, but would also lead to a setting in which the outcome is decided upon by the opponent, as opposed to the UN council, whose aim is moderation and profit for all members.

Given the suggestions above, foreign policy experts must devise a series of steps according to a schedule that provides concessions from the US and the UN with respect to Iranian goods, should the Iranian government choose to comply with UN demands. One must nevertheless reiterate that the forceful military option remains just that, an option, as the urgent disagreement over the nuclear threat, the Iranian influence into the Iraqi conflict, and oil production are yet to be resolved. Thus the true danger lies in human nature, as it is only natural to argue and fight when no other possibilities are available. Even more so in this case, as the many people both think and feel that the current situation is simply preparation for the war to come.

As the situation is multilayered and influenced by an enormous set of variables, why not begin with the oldest and purest form of friendship that may begin to pave the road to friendship? Why not ask the Iranians during discussion with US representatives if the UN could and if their government is willing to accept aid in the form of US business opportunities to establish company sites within the country, thus providing invaluable opportunities to all Iranians to provide for their families. This might seem like a monumental idea, but imagine a soft drink company like Coca-Cola or Pepsi establishing sites throughout Iran. They would be providing crucial employment to every facet of society from engineers to janitors, all the while providing the kind of opportunities that would for the first time in their history make them excited about their contribution on the world stage. In essence, these companies would be equivalent to US emissaries of the modern day, expressing the US's aim at establishing a friendship between the nations and their peoples. In addition to the authentic goodwill shown, such options will not only open further discussion, but any disagreement by the Iranian government will cause the population to stand back and reflect on their government's intentions and their inability to enhance the well-being of Iranian society when the opportunity presented itself. The people might even begin to think and believe that the US is trying to mend the severed ties and may not actually be the "evil" enemy, as they are probably characterized from within the country's borders. To recap, the UN would serve as a neutral body, the ever-knowledgeable mediator that would ensure, to the best of its abilities, that the proposed schedule remains on course, as the outcome will influence all member-nation foreign policy decisions and their respective economies.

In the end, the reconciliation between the US and other member nations, whether alongside allies or with rebellion states, must take place, first to calm the rough seas and finally to ensure some form of stability throughout the region and the world at large. The only way to achieve this result is via difficult choices that in many ways display US vulnerability to all. This chapter attempted to show what went wrong, what could have been done to prevent the war at specific points in time despite the outcome, and most importantly the actions that can be taken right now to bring some form of peace to the current situation and for the future. It also suggests actions to be taken by the UN and sets forward new US initiatives with the aim of establishing discussions with its rivals like Iran, as opposed to the frigid standoff that currently exists between the two administrations. Regardless, despite the goodwill, the possibility of the military option was never taken off the table and remains a powerful playing card, coupled with the understanding that US fighting forces will need time to recover subsequent to their exit from Iraq. As these discussions will have an enormous ripple effect on our collective futures, in every sense, economically, politically, and militarily, one can only hope that these suggestions will help mend the ties between all members and propel all the peoples toward the only common and natural goal: peace and prosperity for all. Then whether the situation calls for a diplomatic or a military solution, as long as peace and stability are achieved, the ends would justify the means. The only problem remains that certain people will have to decide exactly what actions they are willing to commit to and how much they are willing to sacrifice.

# CHAPTER 10

# The Psychological Effect of Choosing an End

WHEN ONE CHOOSES TO follow through on difficult decisions, actions must be taken in order to transfer the idea from the intangible realms of the human psyche to the realism of the world around us. In doing so, the setting will inevitably change, but this is not always automatically accompanied by the mind's willingness or ability to adapt to the new situation, despite having participated directly or indirectly in its transformation.

In other words, if one is to address the current Iraqi crisis, one must first choose the proper course of action for the country and the region as a whole and then take the initiative to plan and implement this final decision, all the while preparing the soldiers and the American people for the psychological tug of war that will accompany the situation.

As there are two options available, we must consider the effect in both cases. These two principal options in question lie either in the current norm, in which US forces stay the course and continue their grinding and strenuous effort of cleansing and securing Iraqi areas from the terrorist threat that surrounds all the forces in the region, or the alternate option, one that appears to be the chosen end amongst an ever-growing number of both Republican and Democratic congresspeople, namely the infamous exit strategy, for which no schedule has yet been decided upon. Of course, there are and will continue to be enhanced versions of these two options, but they essentially represent the decision of this and future governments.

Of the two options, the exit strategy has greater support at the moment with the unquestionably euphoric added bonus that comes with the release of a worrisome, heavy, and unimaginable load. Even as the future announcement will be made, if the US government so chooses, the level of psychological well-being of the American people will reach levels only attainable via artificial, medicated, or nonmedicated substances. The president, either currently or his successor, will be applauded by the masses as though he/she had brought a great victory to the nation, despite the great loss that would have been confirmed after the return of the final soldiers from Iraq. This feeling would even continue to grow, resulting in approval numbers unheard of since the end of World War II. But that peak will unquestionably be met with a dangerous, accelerated sliding effect into the deepest of troughs the US has ever seen.

It will be during this slide and the final collapse that everyone involved will begin to truly feel the obvious repercussion as well as the dangerous unknowns that will rock the US's view of its ability to govern the destiny and direction of the world's state of affairs.

Instead of beginning with concrete examples of the damaged US psychological state and despite the irony of the sentence to this point, America, for the first time in its recent history, will be viewed by other nations, particularly the majority of Arab nations, as the imperialist force that was overcome by the people they aimed to control. In this case, the people are the terrorist organizations who are unquestionably to blame, but then again one man's terrorist is another man's freedom fighter. In this context, terrorist cells all over the Middle East will continue to fight, and the message of US imperialism will be embedded in each and every message addressed to their followers. This view of America as an imperialist state will further begin to sink into the American psyche via osmosis as the idea continues its silent transmission from the Middle East to American soil. It is those weaker groups, both politically and socially, that will then begin to channel these thoughts and solidify the idea into the minds of Americans, while those around the world nod their heads in agreement. As such, Americans and their government must do all in their power to avoid this mindset and push through the notion of America's will to bring liberty and peace to countries around the world that have not tasted the sweet fruit, as opposed to war and chaos as occurred in Iraq. The problem is that the Iraqi landscape will forever be a constant reminder, continually chipping away at America's belief that it can no longer occupy that role on its own or possibly even when united with its allies—such a destabilizing turn of events, all resulting from a seemingly proper course of action.

Another crushing blow comes directly from the momentum that will have been gained by terrorist forces as the US retreats from Iraqi soil, except for some minor positions such as the defense of the US embassy, which will mark Bin Laden's second great victory over a 20-year period. One must recall that it was these same terrorists that took on the Soviet Union in the 1980s and in the end reigned supreme. This battle would mark the second great victory and thus supremacy over both superpowers over a span of two decades.

In this case, the energy of the universe will again be conserved, as the laws of thermodynamics are unbreakable, but at the expense of American belief in its ability to govern and control. The irony of it all remains that throughout the war in Afghanistan, it was the US government that supplied arms and handheld rocket launchers to the Taliban, headed by Osama Bin Laden, which in the end led to the defeat and retreat of Soviet forces from the region. The region then turned into a fiercely Islamic fundamentalist state that ten years later bombed New York City and Washington and finally led to an American retreat from Iraq as a result of aid, planning, and direction from this same group. This idea in many ways will haunt the American public, not to mention those that took those decisions way back then, as they continue to cause destruction to this very day.

Perhaps the even greater danger lies with the mind's uncanny ability to make connections despite the glaze that covers the shiny exterior of the human eye. This danger lies with those that will begin to see a pattern that began way back during the Korean War, continuing throughout the entire period in Vietnam, and then finally throughout the over 5-year war in Iraq. In each of these major conflicts, the US, despite its overwhelming power and might, was not able to turn the tide over a seemingly weaker opponent. The government, despite past experience, then chose to start the fight without the proper, concrete requirements for war, with the current Iraqi crisis taking center stage, as it is perhaps the worst planned of the three conflicts. What these outcomes create, especially with the "exit strategy" in mind, is a notion that the US military has the capability to shock and awe and win short battles, but when it comes to full blown-out war, the military and by extension the people are not able to tough it out till the very end, till victory is complete. This idea is potentially the greatest hindrance to any and all of America's future incursions, including any battle that may take place in Iran if the current situation does not get better. The worst part is that the enemy is studying this as well and will capitalize on this notion through a particular tactic that has come to be the sharpest thorn in America's side. The enemy is now fairly certain that if it can withstand the initial devastating blows and manage to hide throughout the countryside, all the while consistently striking US forces with continual deaths and casualties, thereby extending the schedule required to complete any military task, the US and the American people will relatively quickly lose their will to complete the mission at hand. It is obvious that the American public is simply not as resistant psychologically as they once were in their ability to visualize and overcome their present feelings in order to achieve their ultimate goal: victory. In keeping with the above-mentioned idea, one can quickly build a case in favor of the terrorists, as they have done exactly what was explained above. In fact, despite being in the sixth year of war, one could describe the last two years of the ordeal as a stalling exercise toward an ultimate defeat. Despite the idea explained above, they are by no means directed at the brave soldiers of the US military or at allied forces that have provided military aid throughout the crisis. These ideas are aimed at those citizens, both governmental and civilian, who do not understand that this very manner of thinking is like a cancer that will erode the country from within. These people have to remember that there is a psychological effect involved in choosing defeat, regardless of the synonym used to describe the action. The feeling subsequent to the retreat is the same!

In addition, one must look into the future, and possibly very near future, in which the government will encounter situations where the use of force will once again present itself as an option and perhaps the best solution available. It will be at that point that the blood will begin to rush, as people will make reference to the last great mistake that ended up in defeat or an exit strategy, as it has been dubbed by this government and the media. There is no question that the mindset of yet another loss will flow through all passageways of the mind, perhaps even leading to an offensive front dangerously out of phase with the required response, simply because of the time that would unquestionably be needed to convince the public of the need and optimum response of a planned and calculated strike. The fact that causes even greater worry lies in the knowledge that the enemy is usually aware of this lag and will take advantage of this weakness, as its confirmation will come as soon as the exit strategy begins and will only intensify all the way through to its ending.

All one has to imagine is an enemy openly expressing America's final decision "to cut its losses and head for the hills." It will undoubtedly become a slogan planted in every media throughout the Arab world despite the spin the American media may or may not choose to endorse. This has a nasty effect on the military in particular, as the civilian population's attention span is no longer than a seamstress's needle. This emotion becomes a toxic one and will cross-mutate with other dangerous emotions felt by the military, all in addition to their daily stresses and possible post-stress disorders upon their return. Furthermore, the idea that the mighty US arsenal could be defeated by a bunch of guys hiding in caves and bunkers and behind rocks remains a devastating psychological blow to the US military and the American public as a whole. This one is devastating and adds a feeling of failure, as the raison d'etre of any military force is to defend the homeland and achieve success in all missions abroad. Perhaps the most dangerous and devastating emotion lies in the idea that all the sacrifice, deaths, and injuries were in effect "all for nothing." Obviously, when one compares the feelings of World War II soldiers with those of Iraqi war veterans, the former will always quote the feeling of having done their part in ridding the world of an intolerable menace to society as a whole. That very idea soothed their consciences, and in many ways made them happy and proud of their accomplishment. In the case of the latter, that soldier will look back and see a war that was not founded, a contribution and a sacrifice not worthwhile, and finally a retreat that in essence dissolved any good that could have been achieved if freedom and liberty, at least in moderation, had been implanted in the region.

There is yet another major psychological pitfall that is unlikely to garner significant support but whose realization and agreement is fundamentally destructive to the self-image of the American psyche and its place in history and time. Recall that every major empire over the ages has had its rise to power followed by an inflection point from which it either never recovered or sustained only marginal power when compared with its peak strength. Perhaps the best comparison of America's pattern of power would be mirrored by the Roman Empire. It is during both these periods that the strength of a few grow to unimaginable heights, with control over both huge populations and immense territories all over the known world of their respective times. The US in many ways reached its peak in the 1950s as it presented itself on the world stage as the mighty power with momentum in the positive direction on each and every point of interest, from the virile economy and strong currency to military might and, most importantly, the belief in self as the true power and protector of liberty, freedom, and democracy worldwide. It was at this point in US history that the government and the people were taking the means necessary to create the future they envisioned for themselves and others; whether the others cared to agree or not. This was exactly in line with Julius Caesar's view of the empire and his view of democracy and vision of the Roman future.

As empires, countries, and democracies cannot continue indefinitely on the adrenaline rush that raised them to unimaginable heights, they begin to be less vigilant and underestimate their opponents, at which point a succession of monumental mistakes removes the psychological strength that allowed them to create the future they wanted. One simply has to imagine the decline of the Roman Empire, foreshadowed by Emperor Nero playing his harp as sections of Rome succumbed to a fire he planned himself, of which he lost control. So too has the US, despite not having consciously done so. All one has to do is look back at the Korean War, followed by Vietnam, and then finally to the Iraq war, and one can easily create a case for the succession of errors required for the downfall of an empire, any empire. And for those who cannot fathom the idea, there has never been a mightier, more influential empire than Rome, and it too fell. In the end, the idea here is to alert the US as to its slow and steady hold on their views of society and democracy—that by choosing an "exit strategy" in Iraq, there is a possibility that it has now reached a point where the action of retreat in this and the last two wars will have an effect on the psychology and its ability to maintain its current role, as it starts to see the parallels with the decline of other powerful empires and governments. In other words, by choosing this outcome, and taking the means to bring it into reality, the US is confirming that its "empire" is one in decline and its confirmation solidified by its retreat after 5 years of bloodshed coupled with past losses and is in fact unable to contend with the opposing forces of the region.

It is the president's role, just as it was the Roman emperor's role, to bring psychological virility to the people so that failures can later result in great successes. This is the time-tested truth of a leader, and there appears to be little evidence except for a single candidate, that the future head of state will be able to fill these shoes. Regardless, it appears to be a unanimous decision in favor of a full retreat, and this president had best be aware of the psychological implication of this choice, as the enemy has certainly taken note of the decline in the US psychological state.

If one then turns to the alternative approach, an Iraq free of the stranglehold from terrorist cells weighing it down from all sides, one quickly realizes that in many ways, Iraq is still ripe. It is still ready for conquest. What one must not forget despite the labeling associated with each and every action committed is that there is no reason to feel any shame if conquest and victory, by any and all means, is to be the chosen end. The psychological effect of this feeling is quite simply euphoric and addictive and by no means a shameful and dark act. The only hurdle with the course of action lies within. There appears to be a psychological burden associated with the decision which is unquestionable, as the United States itself is nothing but a series of conquests that created the present union. Note that during any of the campaigns for states, which are in the present day dubbed "red" or "blue," there were many fierce battles with a complete negligence for any of the psychological effects associated with their conquest. If such a project could have been completed for the acquisition of say, the present state of California, why not for a piece of lucrative foreign territory? Why not complete the task, the one that the human psyche can materialize, can grasp, can understand, can teach, and can feel. The effect will produce a state of unease and apprehension, but at the same time will coalesce and align the ideas into a mission statement that can be applied and a result that could for the first time in history place American territory in the heart of the Middle East. As this is unquestionably an offensive strategy, one completely contrary to the exit strategy option, as well as the current situation set somewhere in limbo between full-scale retreat and sweet conquest, one can sometimes be confined to the dividing lines that presently exist. What one fails to understand is that now is the time for a conquest! Now is the time to strike, if there ever was a time, and most importantly for the first time in history perhaps the end would produce a fully democratic society in the heart of the Middle East. This option, being a spin on the status quo, was in actuality the initial premise for the war. This might appear to contradict the more widely accepted view of the government's protection of the oil supply which still remains true, but somewhere deep within the plans was the opportunity to bring democracy, US democracy, to the Middle East. As such, a confirmation will never be provided by the government but the effect of this choice on the mind is rather healthy, as it would in fact bring something revolutionary to the Middle East. If one just sits back and compares the effect on the mind of death for the sake of a consistent oil supply, the psychological reaction is quite negative, despite the intellectual view of the protection of the economy, which makes perfect sense.

So does this mean that one must choose the plan that sets the hearts of the people ablaze? Or are we to continue without emotion, purely ruled by a methodical approach forward, for which the current situation is quite frankly unsustainable? The answer is quite simple, in theory at least, as victory always ends with those who blend the methodical approach with a healthy dose of animalistic, uncontrollable fury. The mind is then "in the zone," with purpose and emotion and the ability to capture and hold any strong point, any people, and any enemy. As is the case, it is unquestionable that to date it is the enemy that has implemented this strategy beautifully! It is now America's turn to choose and, regardless of its choice, understand, feel, and apply the relevant actions, without a thought as to what others will think; and in the end it will be the US government and the people that will have to live with the choices made, and that psychological impact will be felt for many years to come. All one has to do is simply state the reasoning for Vietnam, as more than 30 years later, the effect is still prominent and in many ways indirectly guiding this war to its conclusion.

In addition, one must bear in mind that the effect on the mind of the chosen end to this real-life saga is not simply one that begins or ends abruptly with a choice disseminated from the Oval Office. The effect in reality is the constant struggle to arrive at a decision that one can be comfortable with or at the very least live with. The problem with major decisions or with any decision remains the doubt that weighs down the soul of the person, the people, and the country before, during, but most importantly after it is broadcast to the world.

Regardless of the choice, this struggle has torn the country apart to such a degree that decades may not erase the malice that exists at the personal and political levels between the parties and between the very delegates themselves who feel they have the best interest of the people at heart. It is thus of extreme importance that the future president extend the olive branch to the opposing party such that a cease-fire be agreed upon within the halls of Congress and that the president does everything in his/her power to ensure that the opposing party sees and feels a voice of reconciliation. This manner of thinking must be implemented by the president, so that throughout the process of the exit strategy or the continuation of the status quo, whichever option is implemented, he/she will continually include and even at times go against the respective party decision in order to gain the respect of the opposition and thus help heal the deep cuts that extend all the way back to the 2000 election. Despite all the negativity associated with presidential campaigns, this race in particular will reenergize the people with hope and, more concretely, a platform for which new beginnings can take place. This renaissance in no way points in the direction of the Democrats, but in the direction of new ideas from the new minds at the table all too eager to implement the "right decisions" and the effects of those choices. This will and already has the hearts of many Americans pumping to the beat of what could be, should their candidate of choice rise to presidential power. Again, people must understand that regardless of the candidate or party chosen, not all is forgotten, but the people know and feel that change is on the way, as the new president will have to quickly implement a decision; whether it is a swift reform from a timeline perspective or a more drawn-out approach, it will have to decisively display America's new position on the Iraqi crisis. The actual fight, and it really is a fight, as the arguments are heated with more than a year till election night, will produce options for the American people and more importantly, belief that the new government will have the chance to set things right, if it so chooses. In the end, hope is everyone's greatest weapon, as the mind will equip the body for any end chosen by those in power.

# *The Final Decision*

AS IN ANY PROJECT, this one resulted from many years of continuous attention to the political climate throughout the world and erupted from within, in an attempt to somehow explain the ideas, the passionate stance, that if understood and followed could provide the wake-up call needed in order for the US to take hold of the opportunity that is rapidly slipping through its fingers.

The succession of chapters takes the voter, the politician, and the soldier through a psychological mine field, in which the mind becomes conscious of the decision steps that must be taken in order to provide the final scene, as chosen by the administration and thus the people. In many ways, the goal in its simplest form remains the difficult decision on the course of action in Iraq based on the current situation lingering throughout the Middle East and Washington. In order to arrive at such a decision, one must search one's soul and decide what the goal truly is and whether the country is ready to sacrifice in order to achieve the goal set forth by the government. In order to do so, one must first assign blame to those that have abused power, while taking into account the numerous other factors that have been added and in most cases deteriorated the situation to the current status. One must factor in the unpopular yet key variables that have influenced the progression of the war from the oil factor to the disagreements with the allies and everything in between. Regardless, the context remained from the very start one based on choice. This war, any war, and any conflict for that matter, is a battle of wits before anything else. In fact it is often said that "war is won long before stepping on the battlefield." This statement could not be more true, as what sets people and countries apart remains their ability to see and to feel the intangible; the dream that no one else sees. The ability of all great leaders throughout history remains their ability to infect others with their beliefs to the point where countries are formed and dictatorships are dismantled, all because of those who believed in the end, hidden within the deep dark confines of the their psyches that they chose to showcase to their countrymen and women in a battle to achieve what they rightfully believed was theirs.

The succession of chapters is an attempt to jolt the mind and bring the people slowly but surely into a context in which they are consciously choosing their future, not simply due to the chaotic setting but due to their own conscious decision, demonstrated through their words, their support, and unquestionably their vote come Election Day.

Furthermore, despite the fact that the book appears, on many levels, to represent a call to arms, and this may very well be the case, in actuality it is a journey that began with the idea of setting forth a blueprint to win the war, and then, surprisingly so, through the mix of methodical analysis and free thought, the true realization set in—the notion that victory and defeat were loose terms being imposed on the American people by their government in an attempt to turn the tide in one party's favor. The problem remains that these very terms are not being described in full, and more importantly the impact of such discussions are being intentionally overlooked in the hopes that the hardships of everyday life will camouflage the situation in Iraq. Regardless, in the end, the theory that the people rule the country will once again rattle Washington and force the rotten apples to fall from their branches in the hopes that the new fruit will bear greater riches.

One of the key notions that resulted from my introspection was the direct abolition of the idea that a particular party is more suited for the immense task set before the country come November 2008. If one stands back, one will easily see that there is a lot of smoke cleverly concealing the fact that the two parties are in many ways aligning themselves with the same general idea: an exit strategy on a 1- to 2-year maximum. If one thus keeps this notion in mind, the idea of choosing the party over the candidate becomes a futile exercise, and thus the trap and all the smoke were successful in redirecting attention elsewhere from the true questions: candidates' description of victory or defeat, the schedule they plan to implement, and the losses they are willing to accept, keeping in mind all the sacrifices made by the military on the government's behalf.

In addition to the above, the cost of war was one of the key issues that was addressed head on in order to ensure that people understand the consequences of the government's decisions, and the effect of such decisions on oil production rates that fuel the American economy. This was also tied to the crucial task of reaching the hearts and minds of Iraqis such that their opinions toward the US would remain favorable despite the obvious two-sided nature of the government's effort.

Furthermore, an entire chapter was dedicated to the idea of mending the ties with the allies, in which specific actions are suggested on the part of US diplomats to regain the support of their allied nations. This objective is absolutely crucial, given the obvious military, political, and financial aid that would be received if one were to be successful in the diplomatic arena and is the key variable that would almost surely provide the means required toward a US-scripted end.

At the risk of being redundant, one must now choose to simplify this situation by listing in a step-by-step fashion each of the gates that must be completed in order to attain the end goal. Recall that the goal of this exercise from the very start was based on the idea of providing answers as opposed to additional questions that would give birth to a political/military strategy that would propel the US and its allies toward victory in Iraq and the region. Then through analysis and methodical thought, I found that such a strategy required that the government define what "victory" meant, in the context of the present and deteriorating situation. As such, I believe the ideal strategy, "victory," would require the passage of specific gates in a step-by-step fashion that would clarify to all the plan and thus the objectives to achieve along the way, inevitably giving birth to the predetermined situation as dictated by the US government and its allies. Again this list will remain general, as the specific actions for each were explained in the previous chapters respectively.

Firstly, Gate 1 would require that the government look back in time to examine all of the errors made and assign the blame to all those that willingly put the US military, the people, and the country at risk. Regardless, one must ensure that this action must be completed not in an effort to point fingers, but to note the many errors committed such that history will not repeat itself.

Gate 2, completion, would be achieved once the government and the people realize the importance of psychology and morale of the military and the people. A fierce campaign would have to be waged by the incoming president and cabinet in which the people once again believe that the new objective as set forth by the new government is attainable, that the battle may have been lost but victory in the war is still in reach. The many actions throughout this work can be made use of, but the idea must become a household-accepted opinion; better yet, a household-accepted fact. Once this is done, Gate 2 will have been achieved.

Gate 3 requires that the president decide on the definition of victory and the schedule to bring to life the idea. It would then be his/her responsibility to ensure that all energy is channeled toward the accepted outcome.

This would be followed by Gate 4, in which the president would charge forward and, if need be, use near dictatorial powers to ensure that his/her plan will be followed as expected. With this kind of resolve, planning, and determination, the majority will join the effort because finally the objective will be known and accepted whether they fully agree or not.

Gate 5 will entail the psychological acceptance of both the losses and gains associated with the decision made in Gates 3 and 4. This is a process that in many ways will never truly come to an end, as future presidents will debate the discussions, just as Vietnam is still debated today.

At first sight the idea that the entire work can be included in a step-by-step 5-gate process may appear to be an overly simplistic version of reality, but in actuality it provides an encompassing view of the task at hand and brings to the realization that despite the complexity of the situation, just like any other problem, it can be divided and subdivided into manageable tasks that, upon completion, one can truly shout out in all honesty as "mission accomplished."

In the end, war is a test of will where one takes the necessary steps in an effort to create in reality what the mind has already envisioned. There is a certain strength that is required both physically and mentally so that the chosen ending comes into being, and regretfully to date the odds appear to be in favor of the enemy! Regardless, if the US changes its mindset, its strategy, via decisive action, no person will deny the US's ability to produce the intended outcome and thus prevail in Iraq. Someone simply needs to take charge of it all!

Printed in the United States
117394LV00001B/307-441/P